# DECORATING WITH FLOWERS

### A Guide to Using
### *Fresh and Dried Flowers*
### *in Your Home*

SHOOTING STAR PRESS

This edition published in 1995 for:
Shooting Star Press, Inc.
230 Fifth Avenue, Suite 1212
New York, NY 10001

First published in 1995

Publisher: Robin Burgess
Publishing Manager: Rachel Rush
Project coordinator: Lynn Bryan, The Bookmaker
Designed by Watermark Communications Group Ltd
Illustrator: Stephen Dew
Production team: Simon Rimmington and Alison Guthrie
Color separation: G.A. Graphics, Stamford
Printed in Singapore by Imago

Title: Decorating with Flowers
ISBN: 1 57335 279 9

# Decorating with Flowers

## A Guide to Using Fresh and Dried Flowers in Your Home

# CONTENTS

*Introduction*

## *Fresh Flower Arranging*

## *Creating with Dried Flowers*

## *Pressing Flowers*

# Introduction

*Welcome to the wonderful world of decorating with flowers!*

*In the past few years, there has been a move towards a more natural way of decorating with flowers. A new attitude which sees the floral arrangement not as something to impress with its formality and its cleverness, but something to bring pleasure to anyone who comes into its presence. There is still a correct time and a correct place for those formal arrangements, but the trend at home and even in the office is for a more freer, natural look in floral arrangements, be they created of fresh or dried blooms.*

*The current trend for collecting and creating at home the crafts carried out by our ancestors — folk art painting, quilting, patchwork and stencilling — lends itself to the addition of country-style flowers. When placed in simple, rustic containers such as old tin basins, washing bowls and baskets, these flowers bring a sense of comfortable tradition to a setting. Flowers are an important part of interior design. Together with other natural materials, they can bring a room to life and make it look welcoming.*

*In this book, you will learn about the essential design elements and, more importantly, the practicalities of working with fresh, dried and pressed flowers so that you can begin to use your talents to design and make something with flowers. In the first chapter, 'Fresh Flower Arranging', we introduce you to the flowers fresh from the garden or the florist.*

You will learn about how to choose the freshest blooms, and then how to learn and use basic design skills to create an arrangement. You will find lists of essential tools and materials, and explanations of which color combinations are the most successful for flowers of all species.

In 'Creating with Dried Flowers', the country theme is more than appropriate as dried flowers, more than any other floral arrangement, represent all that is lovely in nature. In this chapter you will learn about the equipment necessary to make working with fragile drieds flowers and herbs easier, and that it is the simplicity of a design that makes an arrangement successful.

In the chapter dealing with pressed flowers, a collection of ideas for making gifts for family and friends carries on the country theme as well as practical advice. This is a special craft, one which preserves the beauty of one of nature's most transient delights — the flower. How a flower press works, what to look for when choosing flowers to press and the many tricks of the craft are also revealed to you.

We hope this book will encourage you to sit back, relax and read about the pleasure that flowers in all their forms can bring to people of all ages. All you need, besides a few pieces of simple equipment, is a steady hand, patience and a creative desire.

# Fresh Flower Arranging

# PREPARING ARRANGEMENTS

Handling and arranging flowers will bring you many hours of quiet satisfaction. The variety of materials that can be used and the arrangements that can be made are only limited by your imagination. Flowers are the most renewable and least expensive way of enlivening an interior room. Often it can be as simple as placing a few gerberas or anemones in a small vase on the kitchen shelf.

Flowers are as important an accessory as ornaments, paintings and books, and more people are including them as part of their regular shopping list. They should not be brought out just on special occasions — flowers are part of our everyday lives.

## FLOWER STYLES

The natural materials available to produce country-inspired flower arrangements are varied and often surprising. A walk down a country lane can produce leaves, branches and twigs, berries, nuts and grasses in abundance. One of the most beautiful and natural posies seen at an exhibition featured no flowers at all. Instead, a collection of hedgerow plants, herbs and oak apples took their place proudly. Even in the middle of winter, with a little imagination, a pretty arrangement can be made of twigs and branches.

The basic steps in flower arranging to assist you to achieve the look you require are in this first section. Over the years many so-called rules have been applied to flower arrangements. People deemed it inappropriate for one color to go with another or one type of flower to be used with another. Fortunately, many of these myths have been quietly ignored. In fact, with the new casual styles — which are the essence of country style — the adage 'anything goes' can, and does, apply.

## GOOD ADVICE

The well-known and respected floral arranger Constance Spry used to tell her students:
'Never forget that in arranging flowers you have the opportunity to express your own sense of what is beautiful and you should feel free and uninhibited in doing so.'

The wooden dresser holds a collection of china, the yellow color of which is echoed in the casual grouping of flowers. The basket is lined with a wired plastic bowl. Sunlight catches the glowing colors of the flowers: Boltonia, *Bells of Ireland (Molucella laevis), antirrhinum,* 'Belladonna' *delphiniums,* asters and amaranthus.

*A low vase filled with a loose group of flowers is ideal for a sideboard location.*

Formal arrangements have their place, particularly on special occasions. Yet even these can have a spark of 'looseness' if you choose the right types of flowers. In general, when considering a design, you will discover that the secret of success lies in simplicity. Choosing one flower, picking a bunch from the yard or buying blooms from a store is a pleasure. It is not necessary to buy or grow expensive blooms to capture a country style. In fact, simple seasonal material is readily available. Often a cluster of ripened seed heads, or a bunch of wild flowers will provide all you need to make an impression. Look also for mosses, which have superb subtle colors and textures and bring the colors of the countryside into your home.

Her philosophy was that cut flowers should be handled in a natural, free-flowing way that recalled, rather than denied, how they had looked in the garden. Staid, triangular arrangements with bows properly placed, even impositioned, on an arrangement were not for her or her followers.

### FOLIAGE

Foliage alone can make a fabulous arrangement — look around when you are next in the country in summer and see how many different shades of green leaves there are on the trees. Visit the same place in fall and see how many tones of rust and gold have suddenly appeared on trees and shrubs. Nature has a wonderful way of entertaining us naturally.

*A moss basket crammed full of fresh flowers and tied with a fabric bow adds a country touch to the traditional living room.*

*This page:*
*A garden bed full of flowers is the perfect place to find a collection of colorful blooms for picking and arranging.*

*Opposite:*
*Flowers in profusion are a glorious sight in a florist's store.*

## COLORFUL COMBINATIONS

Some people have an 'eye for color' or an instinctive color sense. If you feel nervous about your color 'eye' then it may be easier to start with arrangements that blend harmoniously with the colors in the furnishings of your room. Creating color groupings is an excellent way to start.

A simple way to check out color combinations before you pick or buy flowers is to obtain a full set of sample paint cards from a do-it-yourself store and use these to help you match objects in your room and to try various combinations together. When you are ready to begin, decide where your arrangement is to be placed. Consider the effect that you are trying to achieve, gather together the materials you want to use and have fun experimenting with combinations.

### GREEN AND WHITE

Let us begin with nature's answer to the search for a perfect contrast. The combination is restful to look at and harmonizes with most other colors. Euphorbias and hellebores are fantastic examples in this case. The acid green of many of the euphorbias and the lime green of *Helleborus corsicus* is unique. Green hydrangeas have a soft pink blush to their blooms, and alchemilla is a soft yellow-green and has a beautifully shaped leaf with a soft bloom on it.

Foliage of some kind is available all year round. Foliage is not always green as a close look at any plant store will illustrate. Variegated leaves are particularly lovely. Use leaves for their singular beauty, combining leaves ranging from silver-gray green to the brightest deep green for a stunning effect. Most common garden flowers have a white form — check with your local plant nursery. The textures and marking on white flowers produce great variety, so that even a monochrome combination can achieve diversity. Look for the green markings on white snowdrops, or on the tips of white delphiniums. One of the most popular white arrangements is of a mass of white anemones or even *Hellebores niger.*

*Opposite:*
*This small bath-shaped gray tin is a good idea to use as a holder for white flowers and gray foliage. It has been wired to hold the flowers which include* Cosmos bipinnatus, Lisianthus, Queen Anne's lace *and the curious green rose,* Rosa chinensis *'Viridiflora'.*

*PALE BLUE*

*Opposite:*
*An old battered blue enamel jug holds a pretty blue mixture fresh from the garden: plumbago, lavender, gentian, forget-me-not, and tweedia. Such a fresh and casual arrangement looks at home in the smartest room.*

This makes a lovely presentation, from the palest blue of forget-me-nots through to the deep blue (almost purple) shade in the elegant delphinium. Cornflowers, the soft blue of tweedia and plumbago and the exquisite blue Himalayan poppy are each examples of blue flower power. Be careful when using blue flowers as occasionally they can be lost against some backgrounds and do not show well under artificial light. When using blue in a mixed color arrangement, make sure the blues will be seen from a distance — they may look like darker than they really are. Blue does look wonderful when mixed with rich cream, and with white, flowers.

## PINK AND PURPLE

*Opposite:*
*A mottled enamel*
*gray bowl holds*
*tulips, Alstroemeria,*
*anemones, grapes,*
*guavas, aubergines,*
*privet berries and early*
*crocuses. The foliage*
*includes* Stachys
byzantina, Cerinthe
retorta, Helichrysum
petiolatum, *ornamental*
*kale (*Brassica oleracea
acephala*), and the black*
*seeds are* Aristea ecklonii.

Tulips, anemones, carnations, camellias, heather and ornamental kale are very good examples of the types of pink flowers to consider using in country-style arrangements. These flowers have a looseness of form which is ideal for a casual setting. Look for a softer rather than a brighter hue, for this will introduce a delicacy to an arrangement.

Pink roses are one of the most beautiful flowers with which to create a romantic impression, especially for a special occasion like a christening, dinner for two, an Easter celebration or a birthday lunch party. Small buds are prettiest in small vases, with a sprig or two of gypsophylia added for softness. You may like to try floating two or three camellia blossoms in a shallow glass container, half-filled with water, in the center of the dinner table. Place a small purple candle behind the container for gentle lighting.

*RED*

This is the vital color of fire, passion and life itself. In this group, you could include anything with reddish brown leaves. Favorite for a red setting are poinsettias, with their lush, dark green foliage or elegant asiatic lilies, spray chrysanthemums and brown boronia (*Boronia megastigma*).

For a completely revolutionary country-style look, experiment with fresh or dried red chili peppers in a floral arrangement. Their glossy skins are fabulous, even luminous. Sneak them into the bottom of arrangements with similar strong shapes.

Full-bloom red anemones, with their luscious deep black centers, are also fantastic for fall arrangements. Place a group of these in a medium-height glossy black container, stand back and enjoy the effect.

*Opposite:*
*A rustic barrel has been lined with a wired plastic bucket to make the base for this rich arrangement. The interesting bare branches are maple, the flowers are asiatic lilies, spray chrysanthemums and and brown boronia. The foliage used here is angelica, copper beech, magnolia and branches of ripe mandarins.*

### YELLOW AND ORANGE

The combination of these two colors is one of the most cheerful there is in the floral world. It has the feeling of both spring and fall; yellow is the color of spring, and orange carries a feeling of fall. The first glimpse of a yellow daffodil or a tiny crocus peeking through the ground heralds the beginning of a new cycle of life in the garden.

When we see the leaves turning to yellow, then to a rich flame orange, we know it is time to prepare for the chill of winter. But that does not mean it is not possible to continue having fresh floral arrangements indoors as so many flowers are now grown for general distribution throughout the year.

Pyracantha berries, Boltonia, Alstroemeria, freesias, daffodils, some lilies, narcissus, chrysanthemums, small and large sunflowers and pansies all come into this color spectrum. Placing brightly colored flowers in over-designed and brightly patterned containers is not a good idea. Keep the container simple in style and preferably choose one which is a plain color.

*Opposite:*
*A willow basket from Burgundy, France, is lined with star and filled with Pyracantha berries, sunflowers, Boltonia, Alstroemeria and freesias.* Idesia polycarpa *berries and yellow zucchini spill over the front of the arrangement.*

# ESSENTIAL EQUIPMENT

It is not necessary to rush out and buy a whole lot of equipment to complete a wide variety of arrangements successfully. The main purpose of taking the time and effort needed to arrange the material is to show it off in the most effective way possible.

Some rooms, because of their scale, require larger arrangements, but there are also many situations that only require small and simple items. Other locations in a room may allow you to create a 'still life' by grouping interesting containers, filled with masses of colorful blooms, in a monochromatic color scheme or in a mixture of colors — say, a container filled with red flowers on one side, one with rust blooms on the right, and one with golden yellow blooms sitting in front, with the flowers cut to a lower height to balance the scene.

There may be a lovely feature in the room or entrance way which you wish to draw attention to. Placing a vase of flowers nearby will achieve that aim. Display an arrangement of flowers in toning hues on a surface nearby and you will see how much it does draw attention to it. Familiar items can take on a new life when complemented by flowers.

Attention should be paid to shape, proportion, and color as compatibility between flowers, foliage and the container is essential. On some occasions the vase may be almost as important as the flowers themselves. There are many times, however, when the container is hidden by the arrangement and serves solely as a receptacle to anchor the material and provide a source of water. In these instances, a baking sheet can be just as useful as an expensive vase. The reverse may occur when you have only a few blooms, as the container's style and appeal will be paramount and can contribute greatly to the charm of the arrangement.

## CONTAINERS

A flower container does not have to be a vase. The country kitchen will invariably provide a variety of interestingly shaped

*Tall stem grass, heliconia and euphorbia make a striking display in a glass vase. The arrangement is best suited to an informal location.*

*A collection of jugs, vases and bowls from around the house can be turned into items of beauty when filled with the appropriate flowers.*

objects. Jugs, casserole dishes, a soup tureen, mugs, a lidless coffee pot or even an empty bottle or spaghetti jar can often provide just the shape and size to match the material. An empty wire waste bin, lined with lichen and secretly hiding a plastic bowl, can be very effective and stylish. Tin ware is currently trendy but be careful to line the item with a plastic container as water will rust its seams.

Country-style flowers lend themselves to unusual containers. Church and local school fairs, junk shops, markets and second-hand furniture auctions are all good places in which to find inexpensive and interesting items.

The best rule to follow when you are inexperienced is that simple shapes and plain colors are best of all. Unpatterned surfaces do not detract from the flowers. Try to envisage the container you like away from where you find it. Envisage it back in your home, filled with flowers. In addition to finding the right container, it can sometimes be necessary to use some florist's aids. The materials which we will outline in this section can be bought from most florist stores or florist's suppliers.

## GLASS

Glass containers vary widely and range from beautifully designed elegant vases to decanters, goblets, fish bowls and medicine or chemistry bottles. Look for shapes which offer a firm, heavy base and, if they are wide-necked, allow room to conceal chicken wire under the flowers.

A glass specimen vase can be the ideal container to display a single bloom. Choose one with a firm, solid base which is not too tall, as they can easily topple over. A brandy glass can be ideal for a bunch of tiny blooms like violets. Tied lightly together and placed in the center of the glass, they will look very pretty and will last longer than usual in the moist atmosphere created by the shape of the glass container.

Glass must be kept clean and polished. Scrub containers well after use with soapy water, as a spotless vase will reduce the problem of wilting. Watermarks can occur and should be removed regularly, otherwise they could become permanent. A piece of lemon dipped in salt will help to remove stains.

*This poppy-shaped teapot calls out for nasturtiums. You can do the same for any similar interestingly shaped container as long as you match the color and mood in the design.*

*A collection of containers suitable for fresh floral arrangements.*

## CERAMICS

From Art Deco to modern or antique, from fine porcelain to rough but interesting pottery, the variety is endless. Ceramics are usually easy to use and weighty enough not to topple over once an arrangement is in place. They offer the advantage that no stems can be seen and they obscure chicken wire, florist's foam or any other fixatives from view.

Simple shapes and plain colors are, however, much easier to work with than vases with intricate patterns or a mixture of bright colors. If you only have room for a few vases, use only simple shapes and plain shades such as off-white, gray, green and pewter.

If you are fortunate enough to have some lovely antique vases with flowers and other decoration painted on them, use simple arrangements that pick up the colors on the vase and either harmonize or contrast boldly with the pattern. For informal settings, such as the kitchen or bathroom, save the small stoneware containers in which you find mustards and cheese. These are charming for compact bunches of violets, small roses and pansies.

## BASKETS

There is a wide variety of attractive baskets available. They are usually made from rattan and cane and are imported from around the world. Willow baskets are more substantial but also look heavier. Baskets make a lovely, natural base for cottage-style arrangements. Mixed spring or summer flowers in small square, oblong or round baskets on the dining or side table can brighten up a room. A larger basket used in the hallway is a pretty idea and creates a welcoming atmosphere. A basket

filled with a mixture of fruit or vegetables and flowers adds a homely touch to family rooms and the kitchen.

Weave some moss into your basket if you want to create a ragged, informal look. Most baskets have no suitable lining, so a container needs to be placed inside them. Plastic kitchen items are handy - mixing bowls, salad bowls, pie dishes, ice cream containers, yogurt and take-away containers are all useful in this situation. Alternatively, it is possible to put stems straight into one of the varieties of water-retaining florist's foams wrapped in plastic. If your basket is of an open-weave style, then you may need to use brown paper so that you can not see the liner or the florist's foam through the basket.

## METAL CONTAINERS

Silver, copper, brass, pewter, tin and bronze containers can provide the ideal shapes and colors to enhance many arrangements. Rummage sales and auctions can often provide all sorts of special 'finds'. Silver is bright and shiny and can compete for attention with some flowers but looks particularly good with grays, soft mauves and pinks. It can provide a formal elegance for a single bloom such as a rose or orchid.

*The large floral-patterned jug is filled with a selection of mixed blue and purple flowers: Lisianthus, cornflowers, delphiniums, gentian and eryngium. The plain Madeira cake has a wreath of complementary flowers.*

Always clean silver after use and take care if you have to use chicken wire netting for your arrangement as this could scratch the surface. Tin ware is widely available and is ideal for the country style. Try lining the container with foil, plastic or brown wrapping paper to avoid this problem.

Flowers last well in pewter containers and there are many old jugs and mugs with good simple shapes which are practical for arrangements.

The burnished shine of copper and brass containers is ideal to enhance the color of flowers with yellow, orange and cream hues. Old copper looks particularly attractive with fall shades. Brass is very pretty with creams and bright greens.

Keep brass and copper clean and free from water marks. Bad stains can be removed with salt and lemon or salt and vinegar. Rub the surface hard, rinse off and dry thoroughly.

### TERRACOTTA
The variety of terracotta containers available on the market has grown rapidly over the last few years. Flower pots, troughs and urns make unusual and charming vases for cottage flower arrangements. You will need to use a waterproof container inside the terracotta receptacle, or florist's foam soaked in water and wrapped in plastic material. For an outside dining area nothing can be more pleasing than terracotta to offset a simple one-color arrangement.

### PLASTIC
Many people hate plastic containers with fresh flowers but for some occasions they can be ideal. They are cheap and practical and come in every color of the rainbow. Off-white and earth colors will be the least distracting. Bright colors would look cheerful on the table for a children's party with a simple bunch of daisies, marigolds or anemones. They are also ideal for outdoor dining table arrangements as you will not worry about anybody knocking the container over and breaking it.

### WOODEN CONTAINERS
The natural patterns and tones of wood can provide an effective backdrop for a cottage-style arrangement.

Wooden bowls, boxes, barrels and tubs can all be useful containers. A waterproof lining is necessary.

*A bunch of freshly picked dainty roses, some in bud, others about to bloom, make an attractive informal arrangement in an Art Deco vase on a living room mantelpiece.*

An antique silver jug
is filled with a loose
arrangement of beautiful
spring flowers. Although
loose, the display was
created using the basic
design rules, keeping the
height and width of the
flowers in proportion to
the size of the container.

## TOOLS AND MATERIALS

### SECATEURS AND SCISSORS

Sharp secateurs and a pair of short-bladed florist's scissors are well worth investing in when you begin. Ordinary household scissors tend to squash the stems of flowers. Do not even think about using your dressmaking scissors for flowers.

Florist's scissors are designed to make it easy to get right into an arrangement to snip off non-essential material. They can also be used for cutting thin wire. A quality pair of secateurs will be used constantly for gathering flowers and cutting woody branches.

### CHICKEN WIRE

A fairly pliable chicken wire with a large mesh, approximately 2 inches, is useful. It can be bought in convenient lengths from hardware stores.

The beauty of chicken wire as a base is that you will be able to achieve open, airy arrangements easily and can economize on the amount of material required. Keep the chicken wire clean and dry when not in use. The amount you will need depends on the sizes and shapes of the vases you frequently use. Fold the chicken wire into layers so that the holes overlap and stalks can be held in position at several levels. In a tall container you should aim to get four or five layers. In a shallow dish three to four layers should be enough.

Once you have achieved the right shape for a particular vase, keep it only for that purpose. This avoids continuously bending and folding the chicken wire which will crack the galvanizing, causing the wire to rust and deteriorate rapidly. Place the chicken wire so that the cut ends are at the top of the vase. They can then be twisted to clip around the rim or vase handle to hold the wire firmly in place.

To use in a glass container, make a tangle of chicken wire to fill the upper third of the vase, hooking the cut ends over the rim of the glass. Then when you make your arrangement, hide this with downward-curving foliage.

If you are using a valuable china vase or silver container, either line it first with thick brown wrapping paper or try plastic-coated chicken wire to avoid surface scratching.

*Make sure the wire mesh fits neatly into the container you have chosen for your flower arrangements.*

## PIN HOLDER

These are available in many shapes and sizes with metal or plastic spikes to hold the flower stems. They are valuable for shallow containers and for flowers with thick stems. You will probably find that you will generally use a pin holder in combination with a little chicken

*Various items which make flower-arranging easy include a block of florist's foam, a pair of scissors, a piece of wire and a pin holder.*

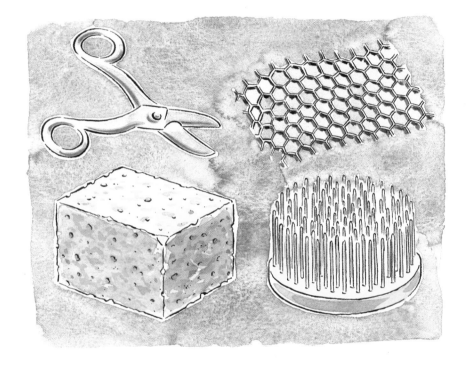

wire. This provides weight and support for any thin-stemmed flowers in an arrangement.

Keep pin holders dry when not in use. Split thick, woody material before securing it, to avoid bending the pins.

There are also small, four-pronged, plastic spikes available which can be used to anchor florist's foam to the base of containers with modeling clay.

SAND AND MOSS

Sand can be used to set posies of flowers in small containers. It is heavy and inclined to scratch the surface of china, so only use sand with care. Moss is an excellent medium. Use it to cover areas of soil in a planted dish or to hide an expanse of chicken wire when arranging early spring flowers in a basket. Always soak moss in water overnight before use.

## FLORIST'S FOAM

Water-retaining florist's foam is useful in containers that would otherwise be too shallow to hold sufficient water. Stems will remain in place with the aid of this material; it is more difficult to achieve a natural look. Florists find that this material often forms a useful base as it allows for easy transportation with a minimum of movement and water spillage. After florist's foam is cut to fit a container, it needs to be steeped in water until it is saturated.

## STICKY TAPE

Sticky tape can provide good support for fine foliage and is a practical support system when using glass containers. Simply cross a few pieces of clear tape across the center of the container and then towards the back.

## DECORATIVE STONES

Pebbles, marbles and shells can all be used effectively to hold stems in glass containers, to conceal a pin-cushion holder or chicken wire base. Some florists stock glass marbles and glass pebbles in a variety of shapes and colors.

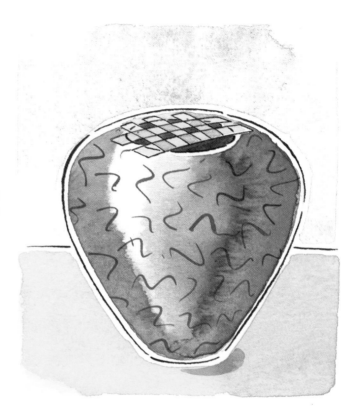

*Tape across the opening of a vase like this one provides support for fall foliage.*

## PLANT SPRAYS

To keep flowers fresh and crisp for a longer period, a fine spray of water from above helps. Plastic spray containers can be bought at most hardware stores or supermarkets. Alternatively, look for ornamental sprays at gift stores and flower stores.

# SELECTING FLOWERS

*A grouping of flowers on a side table looks very attractive.*

Buying flowers can be costly but these days many people do not have their own supply. If you need a large quantity, visit your local flower market. These are generally open very early in the morning and, apart from offering fresh flowers at extremely competitive prices, they can also be very great fun. You begin to see which flowers are in season, and learn about the ways in which they are grown for market.

Before selecting any material, look at the foliage and at the base of the stems. Discoloration can indicate the stem is not fresh. Flowers should look as fresh and healthy as possible with no evidence of wilting. The scent will tell you if the material has spent some length of time in water. The base of the stems should not be at all slimy. It is wise to pick flowers with stems as long as possible then you can cut them down to the correct size for the arrangement. Choose stems which will suit the vase — curving in different directions.

Material selected from a florist will sometimes have been kept in an air-conditioned environment and this will have

*A spongeware china jug is a suitably simple container for a bunch of sweet peas. Note how the arrangement spreads in a fan shape from the central point.*

*A personal vase of flowers placed at each setting is a unique idea for a successful dinner party. Make sure you choose flowers that are compact and not too fragrant as they can overpower the food's flavor.*

helped to preserve them. Flowers and foliage offered by street traders will have been subject to effects of transportation and the prevailing weather. Flowers such as irises, daffodils, gladioli and tulips should be bought when they are still in bud as they will soon open once in a warm room. Look for roses that have nice plump buds with good fresh foliage right up the stem. If buds are not available, then look for

*Flowering shrubs provide strong stems for large arrangements and blooms as bright as this make a stunning impression when used cleverly. Be sure to pick them just before they come into full bloom and they will last longer.*

small-headed blooms. Chrysanthemums and other single, daisy-type flowers should have a hard, green center with a ring of pollen showing yellow at the base of the petals. Poppies open very quickly in water, so if possible buy them with only a trace of color showing. The point is that when you buy flowers they are often all at the same stage of opening, so it is not always possible to re-create the 'fresh from the garden' look. A few leaves and interesting foliage, chosen at random, can help to achieve this look. Look amongst what is on offer for a few tight buds, a few small-flower heads, and a few open blooms.

## WILD FLOWERS

It can be great fun to go hiking in the country and gather material to bring home. Much that can be found is very attractive

*Poppies in a summer garden bed are perfect for picking.*

plan your trip to the country, take a large plastic bag lined with damp newspaper and a pair of scissors or secateurs with you. When you have cut your material, place it on the paper immediately, seal the bag and keep it in a cool place.

## GROWING FLOWERS

Growing your own flowers or foliage can provide many hours of pleasure. If you have only a small yard it may pay to concentrate on growing foliage plants and supplement this constant source of material with blooms from the market or from the florist store. Preferably, cut your plants early in the morning or in the early evening when it is cooler. Carry a bucket of water with you and immediately a stem is cut, place it in the bucket. Do not gather material and leave it on the ground to be collected later as the stems will become dehydrated and cause the flowers to wilt.

and you can devise some stunning arrangements. However, be aware of any local conservation rules that apply to your area and laws that protect some species. Always ask permission. Botanical gardens and National Parks are out of bounds and you could incur a hefty fine if you try to break the rules.

As many country plants have become quite scarce in some areas, it is very important to pick material with care. Never take the whole plant. Only cut what you need and, if your source is a small group, only take one or two pieces. When you

Always cut with secateurs or a good pair of sharp scissors. Make a clean cut and never tug at the material or you could loosen the whole plant and cause it to die. When you have brought your material inside, leave it to stand in the bucket for several hours so that it has a long drink before arranging it in other containers.

Flowers in a window box are perfectly placed for picking. Grow plants which have a number of blossoms so that you can have a regular supply.

# TECHNIQUES OF THE CRAFT

Following is the most important aspect to decide before you begin: Is the arrangement suitable for the location you have in mind for it to sit?

Then, check whether the floral material will be readily available (in season if you are picking it, or in the florist's). The character of your home and the particular room where you want to put flowers will

dictate the style of arrangement to be made. Consider the type of furnishings you have, the colors in the room and the amount of light in the location that the flowers will be placed.

Generally, people aim for one or two fairly large arrangements in a room. However, do not overlook smaller arrangements grouped together or placed on a table in conjunction with other complimentary items perhaps of a similar color. Dining table arrangements do not have to be restricted to one formal piece in the center of the table. Individual posies placed in front of each guest work well. Herbs offer another range of decorative options with the addition of an attractive scent. They can be used in bunches, on their own or mixed with flowers.

Arranging flowers is a creative art. No two arrangements will turn out to be exactly the same which is part of the fun of this particular craft. Experiment with different types of flowers and foliage and different-sized arrangements until you develop your own style.

*Above: An antique chamber pot patterned with hops makes an unexpected container for this cool mixture. The yellowy green of* Euphorbia robbiae *contrasts with blue tweedia, delphiniums and scillas. Bells of Ireland* (Molucella laevis) *add a touch of fresh green.*

*Opposite: Flower stems can be treated in different ways to prolong the flower's life. The hard, woody stems of the protea, far left, has been split. The gerbera stem is cut at an angle. The rose stem has been cut at an angle, in water, and then dipped in boiling water. The stem of the eucalyptus has also been dipped in boiling water and crushed with a hammer to break up the fibers.*

*Opposite:*
*A traditional table setting*
*is enhanced by a simple*
*arrangement of tulips*
*in a round vase with*
*a narrow neck.*

## THE BASIC SHAPE

When you study most flower arrangements, you will readily discern that they are based on a triangular shape. Even when an arrangement is quite casual and loose, the underlying structure is still usually the triangle.

The triangle is a simple design and once mastered will provide you with the basis for all sorts of beautiful arrangements. It consists of different flowers serving three separate functions.

First, choose a selection of flowers and foliage to form the basic outline of the arrangement.

Secondly, add your focal flowers toward the center of the arrangement. These should form a focal point to which the eye is drawn and should step down from one flower to the next from top to bottom.

Finally, add smaller flowers to fill in between the focal flowers and the outline.

Practice with this basic shape until you feel confident with it and then experiment using it as a base only. You will soon develop your own ideas for the style you most want to achieve.

*This is an excellent way to store tall stemmed plants before using them in an arrangement.*

## SUPPORTING THE BLOOMS

### PIN HOLDER
This should be placed in the bottom of the container before adding wire mesh.

### FLORIST'S FOAM
This product is quite good for a beginner as the stems will remain exactly where they are put, but it is better to progress to wire, as this will achieve a softer look. Foam can be attached to the base of a vase by pressing it on to a florist's spike, which is attached by an adhesive substance to the bottom of the vase.

### USING WIRE IN A CONTAINER
Use 2 inch, 20-gauge wire mesh netting as a support for flowers. The correct wiring of your container is one of the most important details. Cut a square of wire mesh to suit the vase you are using. Only practice will teach you exactly how much to cut for the size of the container. Roll the wire lightly from corner to corner, lightly fold in the ends and push the mass into the container. Ease the layers apart so that they are evenly distributed. Allow the top level to rise above the rim of the container; allowing some of the stems to be placed

*A round, galvanised pan holds a rich mixture of red and green parrot tulips and cerise tulips. The foliage includes the pink and green leaves of ornamental kale* (Brassica oleracae acephala) *and the grey leaves of* Helichrysum petiolatum *and* Senecio cineraria.

*The illustrations (right) show how important it is to cut the correct height. The top illustration is balanced; the arrangement illustrated below is out of proportion to the container.*

almost horizontally if they have a curved end, reaching the water level. Anchor the mesh and the container together, either by tying the mesh with string to the handle of the container, or by carefully drilling four holes into the rim of your liner. Thread the wire or string through the holes, loop it over the center, and create a secure base.

Begin the arrangement with your outline of either light flowers or foliage. Make sure the outline is stable, as it is annoying to have important stems turn around when you are half-way through the process. Work with the mesh so that it clasps the important stems. As you work, the stems will support each other but it is vital to have the initial outline stems secure.

If you place the delicate blooms prior to completing the arrangement, you may damage them as you build up the other flowers. It is a good idea to put them in place, to see what they will look like, but remove them before continuing.

Before beginning, place the vase in its final position and arrange the flowers at the height where they are to stand. Raising or lowering a vase after completion can dramatically alter its appearance. Fill the vase with tepid water almost to the top, leaving room to top up later.

## GENERAL TIPS

Try to find flowers in their various stages of growth.
Mix buds with half-open flowers.

Flower stems need to be of different lengths to avoid a flat appearance.
To begin with, keep larger flowers of deeper colors for the center or focal
point of the arrangement.

All the stems in the arrangement should radiate from a center point.
Try to achieve a natural look in the finished arrangement.

Look at your arrangement from the side as well as from the front to check that
it has a balanced look. Do this regularly as you work with the flowers.

Point a few stems slightly backwards for balance and style.

If you are only using one or two colors and kinds of flowers, group them close
together for impact.

Use odd numbers of choice blooms rather than even as it is more pleasing to the eye. If you are using just one or two full-blown roses, beautiful and visually powerful blooms, place them centrally and close together for a fantastic impact. Experiment to learn.

HEIGHT
As a general rule, the height of your arrangement should be one-and-a-half to two times the height of the container. Try to arrange some stems of foliage over the lower edge at the sides and front to soften any straight line.

# SPECIAL OCCASION FLOWERS

*The flowers in this bouquet suitable as a gift for a close friend have been chosen with the language of flowers in mind. Dahlias, zinnias, rosemary for remembrance, elder branches, trailing ivy, spirea and double feverfew are combined with a delightful small soft amber rose, with just a tint of green at its tip. The tie of raffia adds a casual note. This type of bouquet can be eased into a tall vase and it will remain in its form.*

Each year there are a number of public and private celebrations to be observed in every country. Of these, St Valentine's Day, Easter, Thanksgiving and Christmas are the most widely celebrated, with personal events such as birthdays, christenings, dinner parties, engagements, and weddings also becoming special occasions. On the following pages we look at the language of flowers and herbs and how you can use this knowledge to create something from flowers for someone you love.

## FOR THE BIRTHDAY OF A CLOSE FRIEND

A bouquet of flowers for this occasion can be chosen from globe amaranth (a permanence); azalea blooms (temperance); bluebells (constancy); china rose (beauty always fresh); white chrysanthemums (truth); clematis (mental beauty); daffodil (reward); dahlia (good taste); white daisy (innocence); golden rod (encouragement); honesty (sincerity); hyacinth - blue (constancy); iris (message of friendship); lily of the valley (return of happiness); any of the many varieties of roses (love); stock (lasting beauty); sunflower - dwarf (adoration); tulip - variegated (beautiful eyes); violet (faithfulness); white lily (purity and modesty), and zinnia (thoughts of absent friends).

## FOR ST VALENTINE'S DAY

Roses are the perfect blooms of love so take your pick from any of these suggestions. Burgundy rose (unconscious beauty); dog rose (pleasure and pain); deep red rose (bashful shame); maiden blush rose (if you love me you will find it out); musk rose (capricious beauty); a single rose (simplicity); white rose (I am worthy of you); and a red rosebud (pure and lovely).

There are, of course, many varieties of roses grown especially for florists' stores. And many, many more are available from garden centers. A rose can be treated in both a formal and informal way. The foliage, ribbon, bow and wrapping will all play their role in the final presentation. So think carefully about the impression and make decisions on these items with the final effect firmly in your mind. For instance, gypsophylla is certain to give a formal impression so choose a looser foliage if that is not the effect you want.

A red rose bouquet for
St Valentine's Day
created in a lavish
country style is wrapped
in thin brown paper and
tied with a paper bow.
Nestling amongst the red
roses are thin stems of
ornamental nutmeg, ivy
berries and elder leaves
with tinges of fall color.
Such a combination of
roses and additional
leaves plus a natural
presentation is
appealingly different.

## A WEDDING BOUQUET

This is a wonderful opportunity to bring good luck and great joy to the bride-to-be on her wedding day. The bridal rose is the first choice for it means happy love. Combine it with the white lily for purity and modesty. A white pink implies talent, while white jasmine signifies amiability.

Flowers help to set the scene for a wedding day and there is no doubt that the bride's bouquet is the most important floral item. It is necessary to plan the flowers for everyone in the bridal party as far ahead as possible, making sure that they are suited to the style of the wedding and the color of the dresses and of the men's suits. Too often these decorative considerations are left until the last moment and the bride finds the blooms she wanted are not in season or of the color required.

*A beautiful collection of country flowers has been gathered to make this enchanting and unusual wedding bouquet.*
*The delightful September flower, Porcelina roses, myrtle, trails of ivy and thin stems of eucalyptus are tied with a delicate gauze silk bow.*
*This presentation illustrates that you can have a casual feeling yet retain the quality and style necessary for the occasion.*

*The beauty of a flurry of forget-me-nots growing in a garden bed cannot be disputed.*

Flowering almond brings a message of hope and amaranth means unfading love. The beauty of forget-me-not is complemented by its meaning of true love and is an excellent selection for a bouquet, as is honesty, which means what it says. Ivy brings with it a meaning of fidelity and marriage; lemon blossom carries the message of fidelity in love. Orange blossom is also always associated with bridal celebrations as it relays the message that your purity equals your loveliness. There are flowers which carry unpleasant meanings that perhaps one ought to be aware of, and use only when the situation is appropriate. A careful selection will ensure a well-delivered message.

The popular African marigold, for instance, means vulgar minds.

Aloe carries a meaning of grief and affection; a field anemone brings with it a meaning of sickness, whereas one from the garden means one is forsaken, or has done the 'forsaking'.

Giving a pot of basil could be misconstrued by those who know its true meaning — 'hatred'. The same might apply to the giving of a bunch of fresh bay leaves — 'I change but in death'. If someone was to give you a bunch of belvedere, beware, as it carries the message: 'I declare against you' (as does the wild liquorice plant).

## MESSAGES

The meaning associated with the bramble is appropriate when you consider its physical qualities — lowliness, envy, remorse. Red carnations carry the message: 'Alas, my poor heart'; a striped carnation means refusal and a bunch of yellow carnations means disdain. So send those back! Sadly, the meaning associated with the lovely evergreen clematis is poverty, and with the gorgeous columbine, folly. If someone should send crowsfoot, then they think you are ungrateful, and a Venus fly trap is even worse, as the meaning is deceit. A French marigold means jealousy and, of course, hemlock carries a dreadful message — you will be my death.

If you receive a stem or more of hortensia, think carefully about the person who sent it for it means they think you are frigid. Also, the ever-lovely lavender carries with it an unpleasant message, that of distrust.

A variegated pink means refusal and the gift of a pomegranate could be taken to mean you are foolish. A Scotch thistle means retaliation (rather apt) and the perfect plant to send someone rude and impertinent is xanthium. So, you see, flowers are the messengers.

# CARE OF THE FLOWERS

*Terracotta pots are used imaginatively in this tableau. The smaller pots are lined with moss and feature medium-height candles; the middle pot hides a plastic container filled with water for the fresh roses, protea and eucalyptus.*

Once cut, flowers and foliage last for varying amounts of time. Learning some techniques which can help extend the life of your material is well worthwhile.

Whether you have obtained your material straight from the garden or from a flower store, it should be properly treated before being arranged.

## SOME GENERAL POINTS FOR THE CARE OF CUT FLOWERS SHOULD BE KEPT IN MIND:

Always use containers that have been thoroughly cleaned before use.

Always use clean water.

Put material into water as soon as possible after cutting and leave it overnight in a cool place before arranging.

Any material that has wilted should initially be soaked in warm water.

Cut all stems at an angle so that if they slip to the bottom of a containers they do not sit flat on the base where dirt can then prevent the intake of moisture.

Remove broken stems or leaves and thin-out unwanted shoots.

Remove all foliage which will be below the water line.

Spray the air over the material with a fine mist of water to charge it with moisture.

Never attempt to open flowers with your fingers or by any other device.

Do not place flowers in direct heat or in direct sunlight.

Keep flowers out of drafts.

Nowadays it is possible to buy a proprietary chemical substance which extends the life of some flowers. Use these materials according to the manufacturer's instructions.

Over the years some discoveries have been made which, although not based on scientific fact, are known to help extend the life of some plants. It is certainly no old wives' tale that aspirin helps to keep

*A shallow black dish contains a piece of florist's foam covered with moss to make the base for these cheerful anemones.*

## TREATING STEMS

### SOFT STEMS

Flowers with soft, succulent stems, for example, tulips, arum lilies and clivia, should have their stems cut at an angle and be placed immediately in deep water. Some flowers from this particular group exude a slimy sap. Hyacinths and narcissi come into this category. Place those types of flowers in water on their own for an hour or so and then put them into fresh clean water.

Tulips also require additional care to bring out the best from them. Cut their soft stems at an angle and if they are thick, split them at the base for about $1/2$ inch. Remove the bottom leaves and then, before placing them in deep, tepid water for a long drink, bunch them together with their heads level and roll them in wax paper just covering the flower heads. This will stop the heads falling forward and breaking off.

### HARD, WOODY STEMS

Plants that fall into this category should have their stems cut at an angle and then split with a pair of secateurs, or hammered to break up the fibers. If a

flowers fresh and that flowers are known to last well in metal containers. A copper coin in water slows down the breeding rate of bacteria and a few drops of weak disinfectant will help to keep the water the flowers are in smelling fresh.

stem is particularly woody, 1 inch of bark should be stripped from its base before hammering so that the white stem beneath the bark shows clearly. Remove unwanted foliage and stems. Place the material into a deep bucket of water initially.

If there is a time delay between cutting and placing the material into water in its final receptacle, dip the tips of the stems in hot water for a few minutes first and then stand in warm water.

### STEMS WHICH BLEED

When some flowers are picked, a white ring of thick, milky sap forms on the cut surface. Either place the tips of the stems of these plants in shallow boiling water for 30 seconds or singe the cut tip in a candle flame for a few seconds.

### ROSES

Remove all the thorns from a rose by rubbing with the back of a pair of secateurs or cutting them from the stem. The exception to this treatment is for the single rose which is going to be displayed in a specimen vase. Excess foliage should also be removed straightway. Place roses into deep water but, if they are limp, they should be wrapped in a roll of stiff paper

first to support the heads. There are two ways to revive roses that have started to wilt, provided the flower head has not fallen so far to one side that it has cracked the stem tissue. The first is to re-cut the rose stem and split it, place the tip in boiling water for 30 seconds, then wrap the stem and flower in stiff paper and place the stem in lukewarm water for a long drink. Alternatively, re-cut the stems and submerge the flower and stem in a tub of water for a couple of hours.

### SMELLY STEMS

If you want to use a flower or foliage that is known to smell in water, it is best to isolate it from other material. One way is to wrap the cut stem in wet cotton which has been dipped in disinfectant and secure the stem in a plastic bag with a rubber band before putting it with the other material.

### HOLLOW STEMS

Flowers with hollow stems require special treatment as it is difficult for water to get to the flower head. After cutting, turn the flower upside down and fill the stalk with water. Seal the end with your finger until you have placed it in deep water.

## Project One
# DINNER DETAILS

*The completed arrangement is a masterpiece of delicate floral work and will look fabulous on any dining table setting.*

This is a charming exercise, simple to master and adaptable for use on a variety of items. In the illustrations, we have shown how a few flowers, scissors and small florist's foam shape (readily available from florists and floral supply stores) can be used to create an individual flower arrangement to decorate napkin rings for that special meal. Before starting work, consider carefully the colors you should use to enhance the presentation of your dinner table. Read through all the instructions and then gather together the material you need.

MATERIALS
A napkin ring for each place setting
The same number of small florist's foam shapes. These should have a self-adhesive tab on the back to attach the napkin ring when the arrangement is complete.
Scissors
Napkins
Paper towels

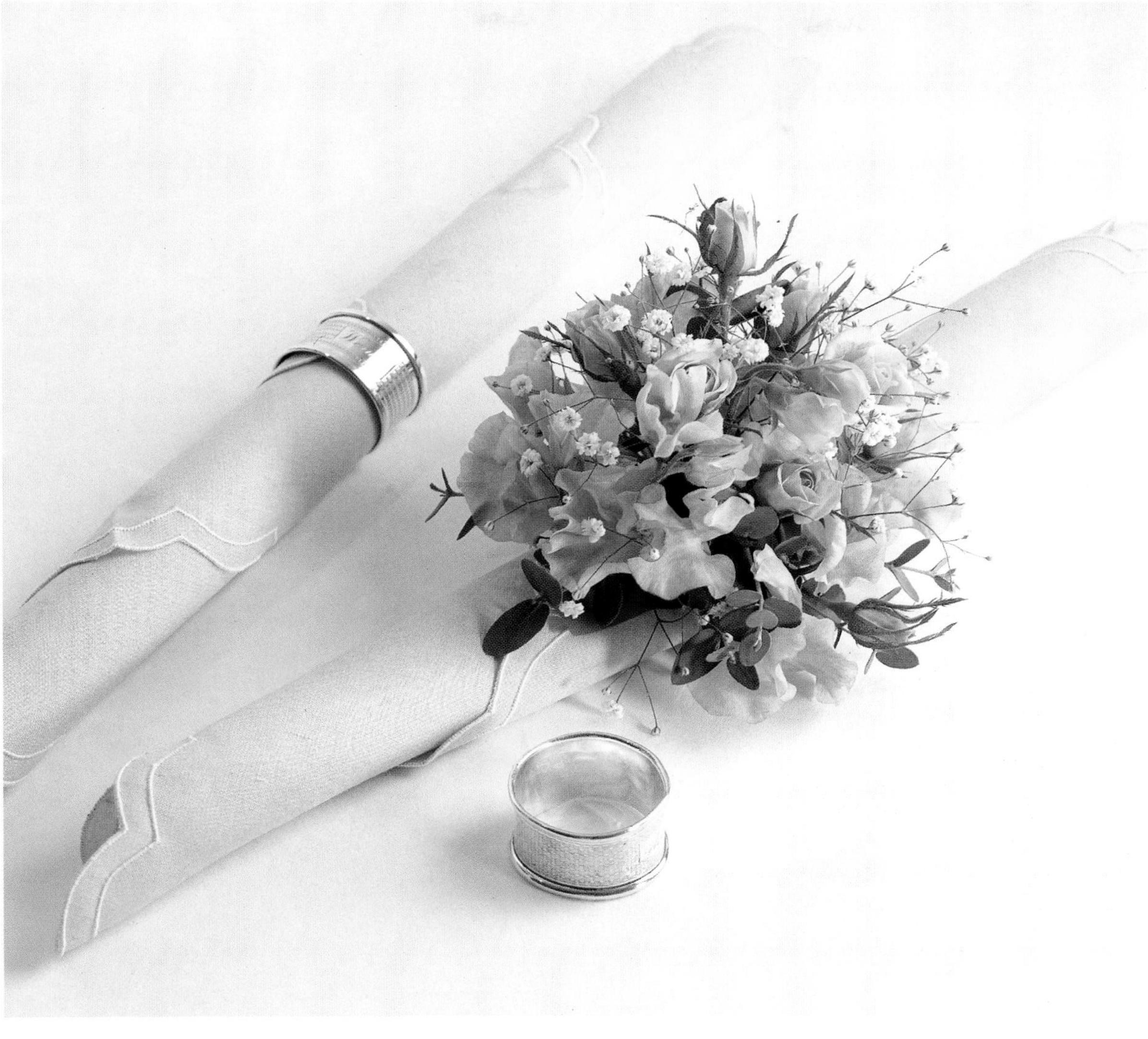

FLOWERS

Some small-leafed foliage to form the outline.

Focal flowers. For our example we have used small pink roses.

Filling/outline flowers. These should be tiny. We have used sweet peas and gypsophila.

METHOD

Step One

Float the florist's foam shapes upside down in water until they are thoroughly soaked. Remove them and immediately wipe off any drops on the underside with a paper towel so that the sticky pad does not get wet.

Step Two

Select your small-leafed foliage and cut it into 2-inch lengths. Remove any bottom leaves that prevent you sliding the stem into the florist's foam shape.

*Begin with the round shape of the florist's foam, add the clipped leaves, then the pink blooms to make the full shape of the arrangement.*

Push stems gently into the shape to form a ring right around the base. Cut your outline flowers to approximately 2 inches. Removing any leaves, push them into the shape so that it is evenly covered.

Add your focal flowers toward the center of the arrangement. Finally, fill any remaining spaces with more outline flowers either of a similar or contrasting shade to match your table decor.

Step Three
Roll your napkin into a long cylinder and thread it through the napkin ring. Peel the cover from the sticky pad on the foam shape and carefully press it onto the napkin ring. Voilà! You have the perfect decorative touch for your next dinner party.

Experiment with different arrangements on the foam shape to easily adapt this project and attach it to a range of gifts for birthdays, Mother's Day, Thanksgiving, Christmas or any other special occasion.

Project Two

# TABLE TALKING POINT

For a formal table arrangement, we chose pink and white roses and ivy trails to ramble amongst three candles. This works best on a long, rectangular dining table.

MATERIALS
One large clay pot( for the large candle)
Two average-sized clay pots (for smaller candles)
Two smaller clay pots for flowers
Two small plastic containers to fit inside small clay pots
One tall, thick green candle
Two medium tall, round green candles
6 yards of Black Watch tartan ribbon
4 yards of green satin ribbon
Florist's scissors
15 pink roses in bloom
24 small white rose buds
12 white roses in bloom
Ivy to trail
3 pinholders
wire mesh

## METHOD

### Step One

Wash all of the clay pots and stand to dry. Insert one pinholder into the large clay pot, then insert tall, thick and round green candle, pressing it firmly onto the pin holder to secure it firmly. Do the same with the two smaller candles, placing them on pin holders into the smaller clay pots.

(If the height of the candle is insufficient, place a small block of wood under the pinholder to raise it up to the correct height.)

### Step Two

Press a small amount of wire mesh around the candle, being careful not to damage the candle. Fill these larger clay pots with lukewarm water until only about three-quarters full, then arrange pink and white roses around the candle. The stems should reach into the mesh and the water.

### Step Three

Place small plastic containers into small clay pots. Fill with lukewarm water and arrange white and pink roses and ivy foliage.

Step Four

Cut the tartan ribbon into lengths of about one yard and tie two bows. Place one bow to the front of the candle, and one to the back, being careful not to damage the flowers as you do this. Cut plain green ribbon into lengths measuring about a yard and tie each length into a bow. Next, attach one plain green satin bow to the left, and one to the right. The idea is to have the bows nestling amongst the roses, with the ribbon ends trailing down onto the table cloth.

Step Five

Trim the long lengths of trailing ivy so that only the best-looking leaves are left on the stem. Place these in the direction shown in the photograph, pushing the stem end into the wire mesh securely. You do not want them to fall out during the dinner party.

Step Six

Lay the dining table and place the larger pot in the center. Place the two slightly smaller pots on either side, so that the roses seem to touch and the ivy seems to meander between them. Place the two small pots at either end in the same way. At this stage, you may like to trail more ribbon through the arrangement but do not go over the top with this creation. Simplicity is best.

## Project Three

# A CHRISTMAS FANTASY

The secret of this arrangement is in the choice of the antique sledge.
If you do not have one and cannot find one, then look for an item with
legs which raises the arrangement from the surface, allowing the flowers
to trail elegantly.

As you can see in the photograph, the flowers are placed so that their
'faces' look out in a forward direction whether they are at the front of
the arrangement, or the sides.

MATERIALS
An antique sleigh or similar object
Block of florist's foam about 2 inches deep and cut to the length of the
body of the sleigh.
Adhesive tape
Florist's scissors

FLOWERS
Red anemones
Perfumed white lilies *(Lilium longiflorum)*
Ivy
Bay branch
Holly branches
Larch branches
Small conifers

METHOD
Step One
Dampen the florist's foam slightly and then attach the block to the top bars of the sleigh with tape.

Step Two
Begin with the white lilies, punching the stems into the florist's foam until secure. Work from the top, moving outwards. Add the red anemones to fill the gaps, placing them together wherever possible.

Step Three
Add the evergreen branches, carefully placing them in between the flowers and trailing the ends to cover the florist's foam. Lastly, add the trailing ivy.

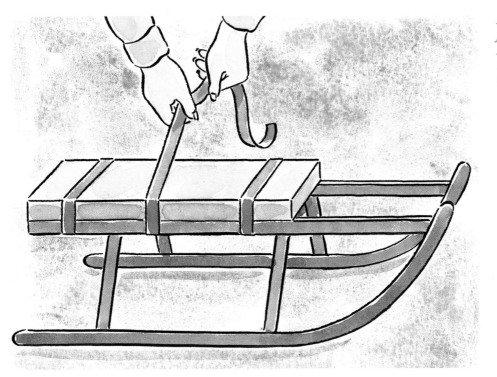

*Attaching the florist's foam to the antique sleigh with tape. This will be covered with flowers in the final arrangement.*

## Project Four

# A ST VALENTINE'S POSY

Here is a lovely idea for a posy for this romantic day, using ivy leaves, spray roses, a central red rose and lace spray carnations, violets and anemones. The effect is unique and enchanting. Follow the step-by-step instructions and you, too, will be able to create this for a loved one.

MATERIALS
Fine florist's wire
Medium-gauge stub wire
Gutta-percha tape
Fine cotton lace
Florist's scissors

FLOWERS
Large ivy leaves (*Hedera*)
Purple anemones (*Anemone* 'Mona Lisa')
Spray lace carnations (*Dianthus* 'Sorentino')
Spray red roses (*Rosa* 'Joy')
Single central red rose (*Rosa* 'Only Love')
Skimmia for foliage (*Skimmia japonica fragrans*)
Violets (*Viola oderata*)

### Step One
Wire the large ivy leaves by twisting thin florist's wire around and down the ivy stem and cover the wire with gutta-percha tape. This makes a stronger stem. Put to one side for use at the end.

### Step Two
Trim any extra leaves from the lower half of the stem of foliage. Take one stem in your hand, then add another, placing it so that it sits neatly with the other. Add the third foliage stem. This combination creates the foliage base for the posy.

### Step Three
Holding the posy in one hand, slowly add roses and the lacy spray carnations, re-adjusting the stems as you do it so that the blooms face out of the center of the posy. This will

require a bit of practice but once you have done it a few times you will find it easier. Wire the stems together at the base of the foliage.

Step Four

Take one stem of violet and one stem of anemone and place these into the posy. Continue with single stems of each until you have encircled the foliage, roses and lacy carnations. Finally, add the wired ivy leaves around the posy. Wire the collection firmly together and cover the wire with gutta-percha tape. Trim the ends neatly. For a final romantic flourish, wrap a length of fine cotton lace around the stems, and tie into a loose bow.

## Project Five

# HARMONY IN PINKS

The idea for this arrangement came from a request to create an arrangement in various shades of pink to be a focal point on a sideboard in a dining room. The arrangement is lush and full of interesting blooms. Follow the step-by-step instructions and you will be able to create a similar effect.

MATERIALS
One medium-sized wooden trug
Florist's foam
A small plastic container the shape of the florist's foam
Tape

FLOWERS
Hydrangeas (*Hydrangea arbor ecens*)
Kaffir lilies (*Schizostylis* 'Jennifer')
Pittosporum foliage (*Pittosporum garnetii*)
Sedum small trailing foliage (*Sedum cauticolum*)
Sedum (*Sedum* 'Autumn Joy')
Pink Michaelmas daisies (*Aster novi-angliae* 'Alma Potschke')
Pink zinnias (*Zinnia compositae*)
Pink tulips
Raspberry canes (*Rubus idagns* 'Ziva')

### Step One
Tape the florist's foam to the plastic container, ready to place into the wooden trug. Trim to fit.

### Step Two
Begin the arrangement by placing the main background flower shapes into the florist's foam. In this case, it is the hydrangeas which are the dominant flower shape.

### Step Three
Here you make the main outline of the arrangement with the foliage and flowers. Cover as much of the florist's foam as possible at this stage and work carefully, trimming the leaves from the lower half of the stems if they seem too bushy. Use the raspberry foliage, the Kaffir lilies, the pittosporum and the sedum, placing each stem between the

outline of the hydrangeas. This way you gradually build up a shape. Make sure when you are placing the foliage that it trails over the sides of the trug (as seen in the photograph). The trick is in the angle of the stem as you place it into the florist's foam. Step back occasionally to see that you are doing it correctly. There will be a natural 'swoon' to these flowers so it is best to follow that line.

## Step Four

Fill in the arrangement with the flowers, using 3 pink zinnias to create a focal point, and the bright Michelmas daisies. Spray the completed arrangement lightly to create the effect of an early morning dew.

# CREATING
# ARRANGEMENTS
## WITH
# DRIED FLOWERS

# DRYING FOR BEGINNERS

*Opposite:*
*Colorful country flowers*
*tied with fine straw and*
*a gingham bow makes*
*a lovely presentation*
*bouquet.*

Dried flowers and herbs have been used as decorations throughout the home from the beginning of civilization. The process of drying flowers retains their beauty; with herbs, drying also retains their flavor.

The art of drying flowers and herbs is thousands of years old. Many people have memories of the faint fragrance of a small sachet of lavender discovered while searching for treasures in grandmother's closet.

Ancient civilizations used the fragrances of dried flowers and herbs to perfume rooms. Rose petals were scattered on table tops; bunches of mixed dried flowers were hung from rafters or placed strategically around in vases and bowls. Leaves and flowers with long-lasting fragrances were often left in drawers and closets to rid clothes of musty smells.

Aromatic bunches of dried flowers and leaves were popular in Europe during the 17th century, mainly to ward off the ghastly smells associated with the plague.

The British embraced the craft whole-heartedly during the Victorian era, decorating their living areas with dried arrangements and their closets with perfumed sachets.

Interior decorating fashion has come full circle. In the late 20th century, with the current yearning for the traditions associated with a country lifestyle, dried flowers are seen in both town and country homes. The style of arrangement has changed, but the flowers are the same. Dried flowers add another option to the wide range of options open to flower-lovers. They last a long time, so they are good value when compared to the cost of buying fresh flowers each week.

Dried flowers are no more expensive than their fresh counterparts and their textures make them especially appealing to keen flower-arrangers. They are perfect to use as additional accessories to the current country-style interior fashions.

## THE PROCESSES

What is a dried flower? It is one which has either been air-dried or treated with a chemical desiccant and sand, or with

*Herbs, including rosemary and bay leaves, are combined with dried chili peppers and cinnamon sticks to create this wreath for the country kitchen. Small white muslin bags of dried herbs, stuck with a clove, are the final decorative touch. The base is made of cane.*

glycerine to make it last a long time after it has bloomed. Choosing which flowers and herbs to dry for display, to make into a beautiful gift for a friend or, in the case of herbs, to store for later use as flavoring in dishes is a personal matter, but it is best to be guided by which plants are most suited for such treatment.

Air-drying is the easiest and most effective method. The ideal plants include statice, strawflowers, roses, larkspur, delphinium, saxifrage, baby's breath, and mimosa, plus grasses, seed heads and leaves.

Chemical desiccants and sand are also used to draw out moisture from plant material. By this method, plants retain much of their natural color, but the end product can be brittle. Desiccants are particularly good for roses, peonies, Christmas roses, lilies, orchids, tulips and zinnias. Glycerine is used to replace moisture in leaves and flowers so that the plant remains fairly supple.

Once you have thought carefully about which method you will use, decide which color grouping you prefer and select different types of flowers that are in harmony with this theme. It is important to follow your instinct and have confidence in your creative ability. Remember that handling flowers and herbs requires a gentle touch and patience.

*Harvest colors are used in this stylish table decoration.*

# ESSENTIAL EQUIPMENT

**YOU WILL NEED A BASIC KIT:**
florist's shears
a sharp steel knife
twine

**FOR WIRING STEMS,
YOU WILL NEED:**
florist's shears
medium-gauge wire
fine rosewire
gutta-percha tape

**FOR CREATING ARRANGEMENTS,
YOU WILL NEED:**
florist's shears
sharp steel knife
various blocks of florist's foam
roll of narrow cellophane tape
medium-gauge wire
dry moss

To sort out the flowers you have picked for drying, you will need a level bench top, either in a workroom, a greenhouse, the kitchen, or the laundry. Clear the area of superfluous items. Always work in a tidy area, and discard leftover blooms or branches as you go. This will leave you free to concentrate on the task at hand. Place each of the tools you need within easy reach. Some professionals like to use a small glue gun to insure dried decorations survive rough handling. Glue guns are available at most large stationery stores.

If you want to store flowers for later use, you will need a collection of flat, medium-sized, cardboard boxes, sheets of tissue paper and newspapers. Ask your local florist if you can buy the boxes in which their fresh flowers are delivered each day. They are excellent for storage.

For drying flowers, you need a room where the air circulation and the temperature are both constant. In the kitchen, an old-fashioned clothesline is perfect to hang bunches from. If you do not have one, then you can have one made by a handyperson; it is not an expensive item. For herbs, or for drying the heads and petals of flowers, use a drying tray. You can buy these at specialty

*Once dried, pine cones can be used to great effect. The Christmas arrangement is neatly balanced by the wreath in the center, behind the two cone trees.*
*These are simple to make; one just needs patience to stick each pine cone on separately, beginning with the base, building out as you go on one level, then moving up to the next level. Use the larger cones for the bottom of the structure, leaving the smaller ones for the pinnacle.*

stores, or make your own by stretching cheesecloth, nylon screen mesh or fine link chicken wire tightly over a rectangular wooden frame. If space is limited, use trays that can be stacked, remembering that air must be able to circulate freely between them. For herbs that you want to keep for later use in cooking, you will need

storage jars that seal tightly. Once you have mastered the craft of drying plants, you may wish to color some of them. For this you will need to buy spray cans in the paint colors of your choice.

Have a look at the wide range and types available at your local craft supply store. Keep to pale colors.

# GATHERING THE PLANTS

*Opposite:*
*A plain small cone tree*
*is decorated simply by*
*glueing dried chili,*
*peppers, clusters of mixed*
*nuts and raffia-tied*
*bunches of cinnamon*
*quills to the branches.*
*The fragile, fresh apricots*
*have been gently wired*
*and attached; they will*
*have a short life, but add*
*a magic, glowing blush to*
*this unusual tree.*

There is a great range of plant material that can be collected and used for drying. A comprehensive chart, later in this section, provides details of when to pick which plant.

Generally, it is best to pick flowers and herbs in summer. You will have to judge the right moment - ideally, just before the flowers or herbs reach their prime. Wait until mid-morning, when the dew has evaporated, then pick. At the beginning of summer pick saxifrage, early roses and Alchemilla (lady's mantle.) Later in the season is the time to pick yarrow, baby's breath, statice, straw-flowers and larkspur. Towards the end of summer, pick hydrangeas.

Fall is the right time to pick ripened seed heads. Watch the stems carefully and when they have reached what you think is their best color, pick them immediately. Once the sap has gone they become lifeless and drop.

Pom-pom dahlias and sprays of goldenrod are best picked in the fall and hung to dry. Late hydrangeas can be

picked then, too. You can hang-dry them, or arrange them in a vase with a small amount of water in the bottom, which will evaporate, leaving the stem brittle.

Grasses, cereals, reeds and rushes can also be picked. Lay them out carefully to dry. Some seed heads may need to be sprayed to insure they do not break. Use hairspray or a similar fixative. Dry these as quickly as possible.

Winter is the season to collect the type of branches and twigs that give structure and texture to dried arrangements. It is best to cut them when the sap is low, that is, when they feel dry. Pine cones should be open when you pick them up. Look for interesting shapes and try to find branches covered with moss. This adds textural variation.

If you do not have access to a well-stocked garden (either your own or a friend's) visit the local flower market early in the morning and have a good look around. Check that the flower heads are in pristine condition before you buy them; wilting flowers will produce unsatisfactory

dried ones. Also, talk to your florist about the sorts of flowers that are best to dry for an arrangement.

## HERBS

Ideally, pick fresh herbs from your yard in spring or summer and dry these for later use. When you are picking herbs for preserving, pick them at their most aromatic. Choose a dry day, as the herbs need to be as dry as possible when you pick them. Do this in the early morning when the dew has gone, and before the midday heat. Deal with small quantities at a time for the best results.

Most people dry herbs to use as flavoring in cooking, but there are some long-stemmed herbs which are ideal for hanging in bunches - for example, lavender, any of the mints and southernwood.

Do not use hung herbs for flavoring food - they tend to get very dusty. However, they do look very attractive in the kitchen, or as part of other dried arrangements.

Strongly flavored herbs dried for culinary use should be kept away from other herbs to insure the flavors do not mix.

Herbs are valued for the minerals and vitamins they contain as well as for the flavor they add to food. Some herbs are known for their cleansing and healing properties. If you have a herb garden, then you are lucky in having a selection of these easily dried plants at your fingertips.

If you are planning to plant a herb garden, it is important to include species of French lavender, sage, parsley, basil, dwarf rosemary, oregano, tarragon, dill, thyme, sweet marjoram, common mint, eau de cologne mint, peppermint, lemon thyme, savory, cilantro, borage and fennel.

## PREPARING TO DRY

When you have collected the materials, do the drying almost immediately. Once you have sorted through, picked off damaged leaves, trimmed odd branches and stems, then you can start the preserving processes described in the following section.

Flowers, branches full of leaves, and bunches of herbs left in a heap will soon rot.

*Far left: Clematis
'Huldine' and Rose
'Elizabeth of Glamis'; left:
Solidago 'Cloth of Gold'.
Below far left: the dahlia
'Ellen Houston' in bloom;
left, hydrangeas.*

## SUITABLE PLANTS FOR DRYING

Some of these plants may only be available from specialty suppliers.
Latin names have been given for easier identification, since common names vary in different areas.

| Latin name | common name | time to pick | parts to use |
| --- | --- | --- | --- |
| Acacia sp. | wattle, (tree-mimosa) | Spring | Flower head, leaf |
| Acanthus | bear's breeches | Summer | Flower spikes |
| Achillea sp. | yarrow, sneezewort | Spring | Flower head, leaf |
| Alchemilla mollis | lady's-mantle | Summer | Flower head, leaf |
| Alcea rosea | hollyhock | Summer | Seed heads |
| Amaranthus sp. | love-lies-bleeding | Summer | Seed head |
| Anaphalis sp. | pearly everlasting | Summer | Spray |
| Angelica archangelica | angelica | Summer | Culinary, potpourri |
| Anigozanthos sp. | kangaroo paw | Fall | Flower head |
| Anthemis nobilis | chamomile | Summer | Flower head |
| Arctotis sp. | African daisy | Summer | Flower head |
| Aruncus | goatsbeard | Spring | Flower head |
| Banksia sp. | | Spring | Leaf |
| Betula pendula | silver birch | Winter | Spray |
| Callistemon sp. | bottle brush | Summer | Flower head |
| Centaurea cyanus sp. | cornflower | Summer | Flower head |
| Choisya ternata | Mexican orange blossom | Summer | Foliage |
| Chrysanthemum sp. | chrysanthemum | Fall | Flower head |

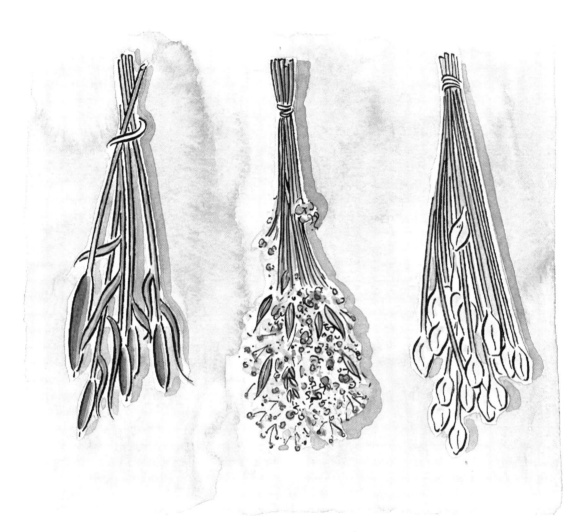

*The correct way to hang a bunch of bulrushes (far left), miniature everlastings, and love-in-the-mist (right).*

| | | | |
|---|---|---|---|
| Cimicifuga | bugbane | Summer | Seed heads |
| Clematis sp. | clematis | Fall | Seed head |
| Clematis vitalba | traveller's joy | Fall | Spray and seed head |
| Cortaderia selloana | pampas grass | Evergreen | Silky plumes |
| Cyperus papyrus | Egyptian paper rush | Summer | Seed head |
| Cytisus | broom | Summer | Branch flowers |
| Dahlia sp. | dahlia pompom | Summer | Flower head |
| Delphinium consolida | larkspur | Summer | Flower head |
| Dianthus sp. | pinks, carnations | Summer | Seed head |
| Digitalis sp. | foxglove | Summer | Seed heads |
| Dryandra formosa | golden dryandra | Spring | Flower head |
| Eryngium martimum | sea holly | Summer | Toothed bracts |
| Eucalyptus cinerea | gum tree | Fall | Leaf |
| Eucalyptus globulus | Tasmanian blue gum | Fall | Leaf, seed head |
| Fagus cuprea | copper beech | Summer | Spray, leaf |
| Fagus sylvatica | common beech | Summer | Spray, leaf |
| Garrya elliptica | | Spring | Catkins |
| Gentiana | gentians | Summer | Sprigs |
| Grimmia pulvinata | bunmoss | Winter | Leaf |
| Gypsophila sp. | baby's breath | Summer | Flower head |
| Helichrysum sp. | everlasting or strawflower | Summer | Flower head |
| Hordeum jubatum | squirrel-tail grass | Fall | Grass seed head |
| Hordeum sp. | black-eared barley | Fall | Grass seed head |
| Hydrangea | hydrangea, inc. lacecaps | Fall | Flower head |
| Juncus sp. | bog rush | Fall | Seed head |

*A large, warm and airy kitchen is ideal for hanging plant material to dry.*

| | | | |
|---|---|---|---|
| Larix sp. | larch | Fall | Seed head |
| Lavendula angustifolia | old English lavender | Summer | Flower head |
| Leptospermum | tea-tree | Fall | Spray |
| Limonium sp. | statice, sea lavender | Summer | Flower head |
| Lunaria rediviva | honesty | Fall | Seed head |
| Mahonia aquifolium | Oregon grape | Spring | Racemes |
| Milium sp. | millet | Fall | Seed head |
| Moluccella laevis | bells of Ireland | Summer | Spray |
| Myrtus sp. | myrtle | Summer | Leaf |
| Myosotis sp. | forget-me-not | summer | Flower spray |
| Nigella damascena | love-in-a-mist | Summer | Seed head |
| Olearia sp | daisy bush tree aster | Summer | Seed head |
| Papaver sp. | poppies | Summer | Flower, seed head |
| Phleum pratense | timothy | Summer | Seed head |
| Phragmites | reed | Summer | Seed head |
| Physalis alkekengii | Chinese lanterns | Fall | Fruit pods |
| Pinus sp. | pine | Fall | Seed head, cone |
| Protea sp. | cape honey flower | Summer | Flower head |
| Ranculus acris | buttercup | Summer | Flower head |
| Rosa sp. | rose | Summer | Flower head |
| Salix myrsinites | willow | Fall | Leaf, catkins |
| Solidago canadensis | golden rod | Fall | Spray |
| Sphagnum sp. | sphagnum moss | Summer | Leaf |
| Stachys lantana | lamb's ear | Summer | Leaf |

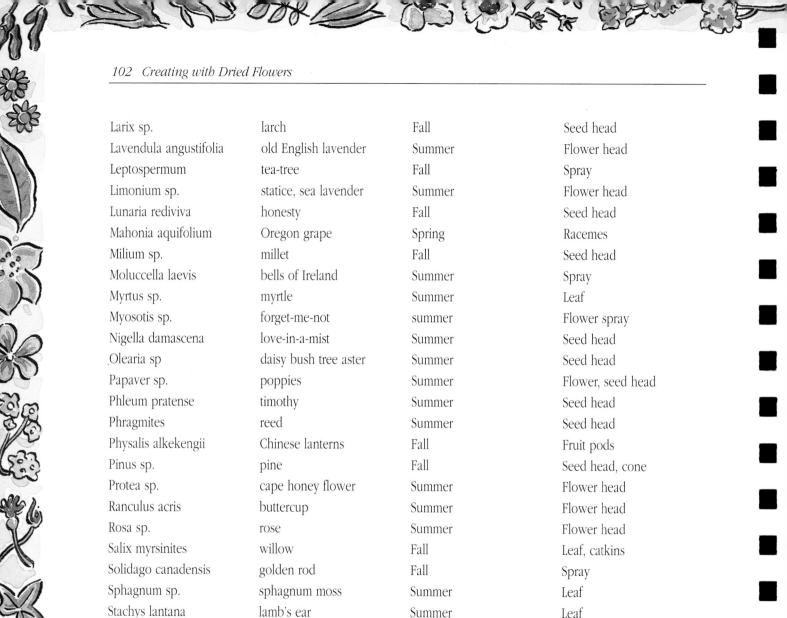

*For creating a dried flower display, choose a box like this and fill the compartments with the flowers you love.*

# TECHNIQUES OF THE CRAFT

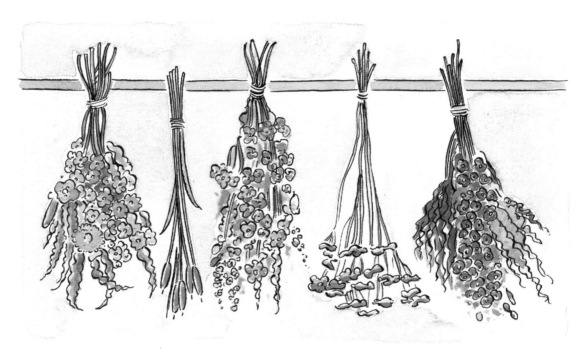

## AIR-DRYING

The simplest and most popular method of drying plants and herbs is air-drying. All you need is a dry, cool room (where the temperature is constant), with good air circulation. Most flowers can be hung in bunches.

To hang, strip the first 4 inches of each stem and tie the flowers together with string. Bunch loosely and make sure there is enough air circulating around the plants or they will rot. Some plants can be dried lying flat, others can stand upright in a vase.

## FLAT DRYING

Grasses, fungi, twigs and bamboo are suitable for drying flat. Their leaves will shrink but they will keep their natural shape and color on the stem.

It is important to lay the plants on a surface which will absorb moisture - newspaper and posterboard are excellent. Leave a lot of space around the plants for air circulation. There are two ways to dry plants standing upright in a vase.

Some tall grasses and seed heads like pampas, dock, bulrushes and sea lavender dry well when just left in a dry and empty vase.

Hydrangea, mimosa, gypsophila and delphinium will dry better if stood in about 2 inches of water. The water evaporates (after being absorbed by the plant stem) and the plant dries out.

You can also dry leaves and petals separately. Rose petals, lemon verbena, scented geraniums or whole flower heads without their stems will dry if they are placed in a single layer on a drying tray.

The drying time for flowers varies from 2 to 10 days, depending upon the humidity and the amount of moisture in the leaves.

*An old pottery jug holds a generous mass of Solidaster luteus (a cross between golden rod and aster) and a few wild grass seeds. The narrow neck allows the stems to stand tall.*

## HERBS

Herbs sometimes take up to two weeks to dry. For herbs, the air must be able to circulate around them and it is best to keep individual herbs separate when drying so that their aromas do not become mixed. Spread the herb sprigs and petals evenly over trays lined with sheets of an absorbent paper (newspaper or plain

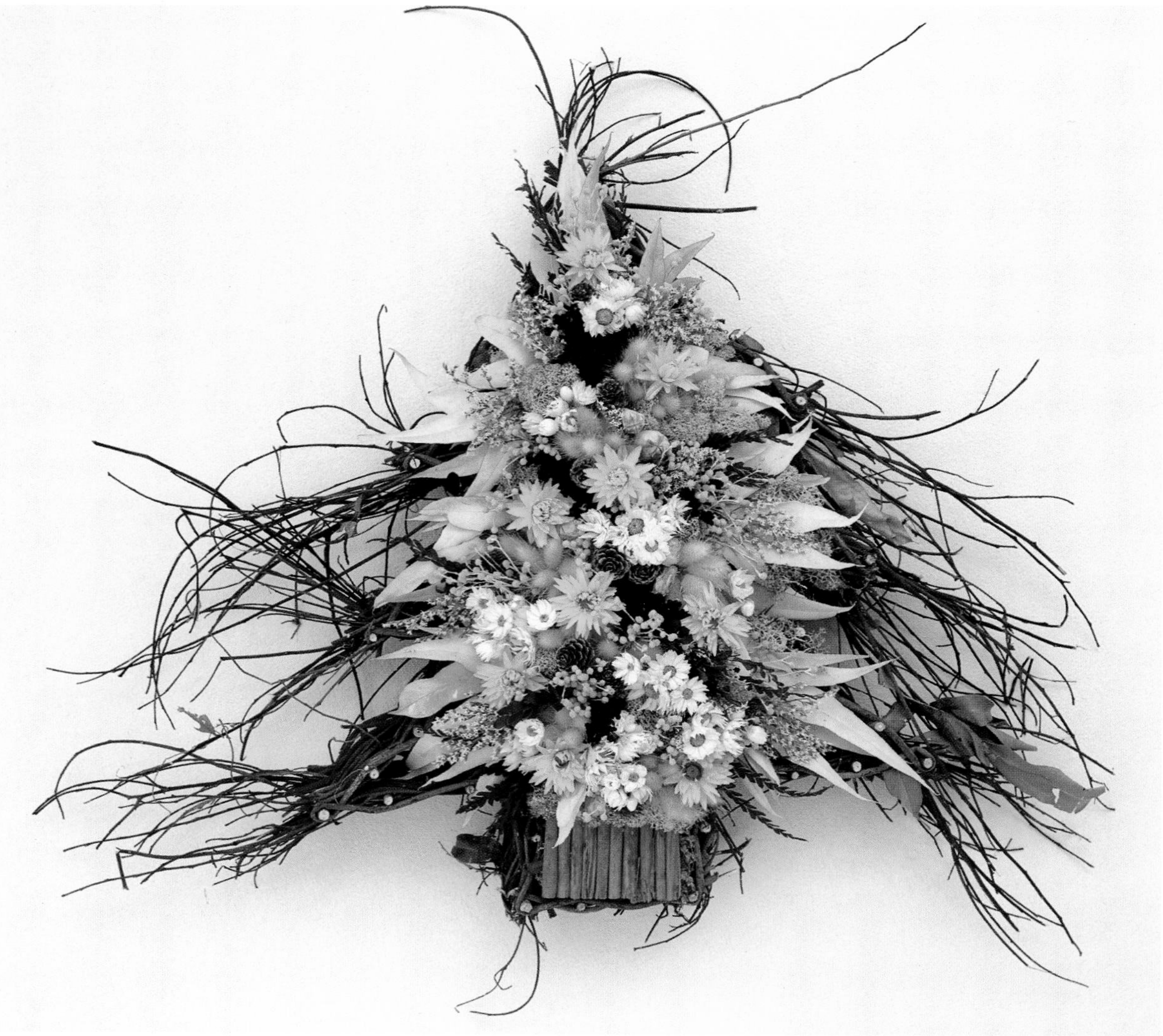

paper towels). For large-leaved plants, such as lovage and comfrey, remove the leaves from the sprigs before you dry them. Check herbs regularly, turning them over daily, until you feel they are crisp. When they are completely dry, place the herbs in an airtight container. Label the jar and store it in a dark closet.

If the weather is damp, try this alternative method, but do it with care. Place herbs or petals on a baking sheet and put them in the oven, at your oven's lowest temperature. It is best to leave the oven door open slightly. The faster the plants dry, the more fragrance and color they retain, especially the herbs.

If you dry herbs on a regular basis, it is worth making a drying frame. Stretch a piece of muslin or fine netting over a rectangular wooden frame and lay the herbs on this muslin to dry. More than one frame can be used. If you use three or more, then the frames can be stacked one on top of the other as long as you leave about 2 inches between the frames. You can speed up the process by placing the trays or frames in a warm airing cupboard for three to four days.

Herb flowers, such as camomile, feverfew, lavender, sorrel or tansy, and sprigs such as rosemary, sage or bay, can be air-dried in bunches. Tie four to five herb sprigs loosely into a bunch by the stems, using string, and hang them upside down in a dry, well-ventilated room where the temperature remains constant, keeping them out of direct sunlight.

When drying herbs with large flower heads, such as chives, the flowers must rest on a wire mesh with the stems hanging

*Flower heads dry well when hung through a wire mesh screen. You can buy mesh trays ready made, or you can make one yourself using a timber frame with fine wire mesh stretched across.*

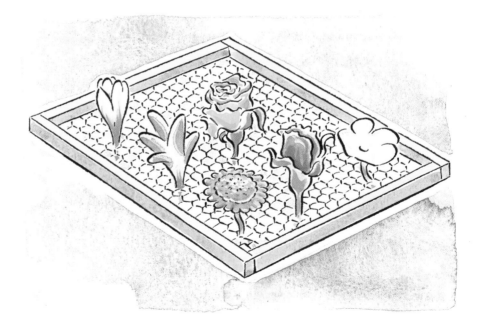

*A mixture of dried material in a contemporary style. The colors are the most important elements here. The glazed container reflects the glazed fruits which you can see in the topiary arrangement. The bows on either side provide the decorative finish.*

heads, such as fennel, lovage and caraway, and large herbs such as angelica, can be dried standing upright in empty tall vases.

## MICROWAVE DRYING

If you have a microwave, place two sheets of paper towel on the turntable, spread out the leaves and petals on top and cover with two more paper towels.

Set the microwave on high for 1 minute, although some herbs may take longer. Check frequently and as soon as they are

*A mixture of wheat, oats, barley and quaking grass in a biodegradable planter. The restful colors are particularly suitable for the corner of this room.*

Set the microwave on high for 1 minute, although some herbs may take longer. Check frequently and as soon as they are crisp, place in a jar, label and store.

## DRYING MOSS IN A BOX

All mosses dry well in a box. Lay the moss in a single layer on a mass of crumpled newspaper in a box. Pack it loosely so the air can circulate or the moss will rot. Dry sphagnum moss, lichen and selaginella can all be dried using this method.

## CONES

Cones start drying while they are on the tree. Collect well-shaped cones from the ground and place them in a large basket or wooden bowl so that air can reach into the scales. Turn them occasionally and, when there is no moisture between scales, they are dry.

## USING GLYCERINE

If you use glycerine to preserve plant leaves and other material, you will need to discover the advantages and disadvantages. With glycerine, the material remains supple, however, leaves and flowers change color and usually become a pale, dull, brown shade.

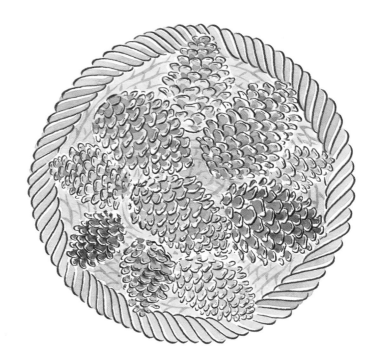

The method involves placing material in a mixture of glycerine and water. The plant absorbs the mixture and the water gradually evaporates, leaving the plant saturated with the glycerine. In preparation for this process, strip the end of the stem of leaves and cut the stem at a sharp angle. Hardwood stems should be split and hammered. A typical glycerine mixture consists of 40 percent glycerine to

*Drying pine cones is a matter of placing them in a deep bowl, ensuring a good supply of air around them.*

*Preserve leaves in a
half and half mixture
of glycerine and water
to make them pliable.*

60 percent hot water. Pour the mixture into a suitable vase to a depth of 4 inches and place the stems in vase. Keep this in a cool, dark place during absorption. Check the progress after a week.

To preserve good-sized leaves, place half-and-half glycerine/water mixture in a wide open bowl. Soak the leaves until the color changes completely, then remove from the mixture. Wash them in a mild detergent and lay them flat on sheets of newspaper to dry. These leaves will remain pliable for some time and a collection of leaves is handy when planning wreaths and other decorative items. Ivy, magnolia, aspidistra and eucalyptus leaves respond well to this method of preservation.

## USING DESSICANTS
A dessicant is a drying agent. Silica gel, borax and sand, or a mixture of the three, are the most common agents used to absorb the water content from leaves and flowers. This method retains a freshness of form and color.

## SILICA GEL
This dries material quickly and it can be used again and again. Pharmacies stock it is the form of white crystals and as crystals with a color indicator. The latter are blue when dry and turn pink when they have absorbed water. It is important to grind the crystals to at least half of their original size before use.

*Delicate dried rose buds have been carefully made into this gorgeous topiary.*
*Adding the rose buds to the terracotta container is an inspired finishing touch.*

**Fig. 1 (above)**
Use a container that can be sealed tightly, for instance, a cookie tin. Place a layer of crystals about 1/2 inch thick on the bottom of the container.

**Fig. 2 (above, right)**
Lay flower heads or leaves on top, adding more crystals.

**Fig. 3 (right)**
Make sure the crystals find their way between petals (use a small paintbrush to help them in) and cover the flowers and leaves completely.

Fig. 4 (above)
Seal the container.

Fig. 5 (above, right)
Open it after 2 days and the material
should be firm to touch. By this time
the color indicator should have changed
color. Remove the plant material as soon
as it is dry or it will become brittle and
break easily.

*The following pages:
A scene from a dried
flower workroom
includes wreath bases,
herbs and flowers
hanging to dry, and a
collection of household
implements useful in the
drying process.*

*A mixture of preserved foliage of a brilliant fall arrangement. This copper casserole dish looks wonderful with the darker foliage colors. The leaves are of magnolia, oak, silver dollar gum and copper beech.*

## BORAX AND SAND

Borax is a powder which is best mixed with a fine, dry sand. As a rule, mix three parts of chemical to two parts of sand. Use the combination in the same way as for silica gel but wait at least 10 days before checking to see if the flowers and leaves are dry. Dessicants are good for use on: roses, poenies, zinnias, delphiniums, gentians, hellebores, small dahlias, larkspurs, orchids and narcissi.

## STORING DRIED MATERIAL

You can store dried material for several months without it deteriorating. The most attractive way to store bunches is by hanging them in a room, either from the ceiling or on a wall. Otherwise, you can store them in large, flat boxes.

Make loose bunches and place in a box in layers. It is important to support fragile flower heads with crumpled tissue or newspaper. Delicate flower heads like roses, should be wrapped singly for better protection.

Do not mix preserved material with dried materials as the moisture will cause the former to rot. Store any boxed material in a dry place and, if you use a closet, make sure it is well ventilated.

*Creating a small tableau
in a corner of a room
can add a country touch
to a decorating scheme.*

*A bouquet created in fall tones features, among other plants, dried roses, oat grass, golden rod, and gypsophila. The green taffeta bow completes the bouquet.*

Many of the flowers and bunches of leaves you have chosen to dry will need to be wired to make up for a shortness of stem, or to make the arrangement less fragile.

Stub wire is ideal for this, as it is flexible and strong, and rose wire is excellent to bind. Use gutta-percha tape to disguise the wire.

## WIRING A SINGLE FLOWER

1  Cut off flower head, leaving about
1 inch of stem.

2  Hold stub wire so it touches the base
of the flower and is next to stem. Wind a
length of fine rose wire around stub wire
and stem. Wind down the stub wire for
about 3 inches. Cut rose wire and fold in
carefully.

3  Hold flower head upside down, place
the end of gutta-percha tape behind the
stem on the diagonal. Keeping the tape
taut, wind this down in a spiral to cover
the wires. Cut it and neatly fold in the
ends.

*Opposite:*
*A vision of splendor - a mass of Solidago 'Laurin' waiting to be picked and hung in bunches to dry plant to use in country-style dried arrangements. Remember the blooms will fade a little but they will still be most attractive, adding a soft and fluid movement to your display.*

## WIRING BUNCHES

Use a lengthy piece of medium-gauge stub wire and place it next to the stem ends. About 2 ins up the stem, bend one end of the wire around behind the group of stems and down to the length of the group of stems.

Continue winding the long end left down over the stems and the short wire piece, so that what is left (the longer end) becomes an extension of the flower stems.

# MAKING POTPOURRI

*Opposite:*
*A bowl of rose petals*
*makes a good base*
*for a potpourri.*

Potpourris are one of the oldest ways to perfume a house. Fragrances have scented palaces and churches since the beginning of what we know as civilization. Closely linked with religious practices (frankincense and myrrh are mentioned in the Bible) and practical needs, perfumes have gradually evolved according to the availability of ingredients and, to an increasing extent, to the demands of fashion.

By the early 16th century, European herbalism was certainly well established, not only for the production of fragrances but also for the manufacturing of potions to cure illness and ward off evil and diseases.

Now you see so many different aromatic potpourris on sale in department and specialty stores, complete with oils and packaged in elegant containers that the origins of potpourri have almost been lost.

Genuine hand-made potpourris have a unique rich fragrance which is impossible to re-create artificially. Sometimes made of up to twenty natural ingredients, you will

rarely find two mixtures which smell the same. These original potpourris speak as much of the person who created them as they do about the garden from which they were sourced.

Ecological and recyclable, potpourris are the ultimate 'green' perfuming product: once established, they can last for years with the help of some carefully chosen additions from season to season.

Potpourris contain scented and unscented materials of various colors and shapes. They also contain essential oils which are largely non-floral in their origin. (If adding oils, ensure you buy pure essential oils, not artificial ones as these will not have the same intensity of fragrance. These oils are strong and should be kept well out of the way of young children. Allergies do occur with these natural ingredients, so please take care when handling them.)

'Fixing' the material is an important aspect of making a potpourri. These absorb and retain the volatile scented oils that give the mixture its strongest perfume. Orris root powder (eight teaspoons per

*Dried roses scattered on a tabletop.*

*Here is a lovely way to present a gift of potpourri to someone you love. Fill a charming balsa wood box with the potpourri mixture, decorate the lid with bows, shells or anything appropriate. The beauty of these boxes is the lids allow the fragrance of the mixture to filter through to the room. This box is perfect for placing in a wardrobe or in a drawer to keep clothes smelling fresh.*

pound of dried floral material) and gum benzoin are the easiest to obtain and are the most commonly used for the process. Other fixatives are frankincense, myrrh, sweet flag root, musk seed, oil of sandalwood, cassia and cedarwood. Some kitchen herbs and spices double as fixative: cinnamon powder, cloves, nutmeg, cumin, coriander, sweet cicily seeds, angelica seeds, camomile flowers and vanilla pods.

Dry potpourris can be made from any combination of colorful and fragrant flowers, herbs, and spices.

## FOR COLOR
cornflowers, roses, marigolds, pansies

## FOR FRAGRANCE
bergamot, chamomile, carnations, violets, lavender, jasmine, mimosa, honeysuckle, pinks

## FOR SPICE
allspice, cardamom, cinnamon, cloves, ginger, mace

## SCENTED LEAVES
basil, eucalyptus, bay, lemon balm, myrtle, roses, geraniums, thyme, rosemary

Most suppliers offer a mail-order service and stock a wide range of materials, so it is a good idea to send away for a catalogue.

## MAKING AND DISPLAYING POTPOURRI
Containers play a vital role in creating the character of the mixture. Original potpourri vessels and jars were developed around the 1700s and because they were so admired, their designs evolved into an elaborate art form. Some of the early pomanders are exquisitely made and are the perfect way to store and display potpourri.

There are two basic ways to make a potpourri - the dry and the moist methods.

The moist method is the original, more highly fragranced potpourri; the dry is quicker and more commonly used as it is visually appealing.

*Clear bags of potpourri, tied with a pretty ribbon, make ideal gifts.*

The essential equipment consists of things you can find in the kitchen:
a small mixing bowl
metal and wooden spoons
a large mixing bowl
notebook and pen
air-tight container
pipettes
large storage jar
eye-droppers

## EQUIVALENT MEASURES
You may find these helpful if you are translating from old recipes.
1/2 teaspoon = 2.5ml
1 teaspoon = 5ml
3 teaspoons = 1 tablespoon/15ml
16 tablespoons = 1 cup (225ml/ 8fl oz)
1 cup = 1 handful

60 drops essential oil = 1 teaspoon
30g/1oz spices or fixative = 1/3 cup
30g/1oz dried herbs = 3/4 cup
30g/1oz small petals or flowers = 1 cup
30g/1oz large petals or rose buds = 1 cup

## DRY METHOD
### DRY POTPOURRI PROPORTIONS
1 tablespoon spice to 4 cups of petals
1/3 cup fixative to 4-8 cups of petals
4-6 drops essential oils to 6-8 cups
of petals

Making the mixture is simple if you follow these instructions. Gather all of your dried material, the fixatives and oils on a flat working surface before you begin.

1. Place the ground spices and fixatives in a small bowl.

2. Add the essential oil and rub between your fingers until well blended.

3. Place the other dry ingredients into a large bowl and mix well. Then stir in the first mixture.

4. Place the finished mix into an air-tight container and leave in a cool, dark place for 4-6 weeks. The longer it is left, the stronger the aroma.

5. Transfer the mixture into the display container and decorate.

*In Europe and the East in the 13th century, piquant pomanders were carried by people through their every day lives to ward off the evils of disease and body odor. Today, these spicy creations are usually decorative. These pomanders, covered in fine muslin and tied with a cute bow, make an ideal gift at Christmas time.*

## MOIST METHOD
MOIST POTPOURRI PROPORTIONS
1 cup salt to 3 packed cups fresh petals
1/3 cup fixative to 4-8 cups dried petals
4-6 drops essential oils to 6-8 cups of
dried petals

Moist potpourris are made using partially dried plant materials, the only criterion being a strong scent. In the past only fragrant roses were used. Popular herbal ingredients include bay, thyme, rosemary and mint. The most used spices are ground cloves, allspice and crushed cinnamon.

## Stage One — Making the Stock

1. Using two-day dry rose petals, make a layer in the bottom of an air-tight jar.

2. Sprinkle a layer of coarse salt (this can be mixed with brown sugar and a few drops of brandy) on top of the petals.

3. Add another layer of petals, alternating with the salt until the jar is full, pressing each layer down well.

4. Seal the jar and leave to cure for two months in a dry, cool place, draining off any excess liquid that collects.

## Stage Two — The Dry Stage

1. After the curing time has passed, take out the resultant mixture from the jar and crumble it into a bowl.

2. Add the remaining dried plant ingredients, spices and fixative.
3. Store in an airtight jar for 2-3 weeks.

4. Add the essential oil of your choice and then display in a decorative container with a perforated and close-fitting lid.

CLASSIC ROSE BOWL
An elegant mixture of roses, enhanced by the sweet perfume of the tonka bean made using the dry method.

## Ingredients
6 cups rose petals
3 cups rose leaves
3 cups lavender
1/2 cup baby bay leaves
4 tablespoons ground cinnamon
3 tablespoons allspice
3 tablespoons ground cloves
2oz ground tonka bean
2 oz orris root powder
5 drops rose oil
3 drops lavender oil

PEACH PERFUME
A soothing, gently scented summer mix ideal for the bedroom, made using the dry method.

## Ingredients
2 cups peach and cream rose petals
1 cup globe amaranth
1 cup dried peach slices
1/2 cup dried apple rings
1 cup lemon grass
1/2 cup willow catkins
1 cup mixed lemon balm, thyme, mint
        and marjoram
1/2 tablespoon ground cloves
1/2 tablespoons allspice
10z orris root powder
2 drops peach oil
2 drops vanilla oil
2 drops rose oil

AROMATIC WOODLAND
This sharp, fiesty potpourri has a festive, woody theme and is made using the dry method.

## Ingredients
4 cups mixed alder cones, small pine
        cones, larch cones, Monterey
        and cedar petals
2 cups red wood curls
2oz whole mace
2oz whole nutmeg
1 teaspoon ground allspice
2 teaspoon ground cinnamon
1oz gum benzoin powder
2 drops lavender oil
2 drops pine oil
2 drops lemon oil

Items from a woodland walk will make an interesting potpourri when combined with smaller dried leaves and blooms. The shell is an interesting container and will suit a bathroom setting.

# MAKING A WREATH

*Natural straw wreath bases are available in a few colors and can be simply decorated by tying the dried flowers around the wreath as you make it. Use a fine natural twine or florist's wire. Keep the decoration in the style of the wreath base. This is not the situation where you would use delicate dried rose buds, or similarly elegant romantic dried flowers. These are country wreaths and are best as a base for wild flowers or herbs.*

The wreath was one of the earliest home decorating traditions, especially popular at festive times such as Thanksgiving and Christmas. There are a variety of bases and shapes to choose from for a wreath. The base you decide upon will dictate the style of wreath. You may decide to decorate only a small part of a circle or heart, leaving the beauty of the base to show through. Many of the grape or honeysuckle vines are especially attractive with a cleverly placed decoration and bow.

## BASES FOR A WREATH

Buy a wire frame from a florist or ready-made straw shape; use grapevine, honeysuckle, or wisteria vine. If you want to try your hand at a vine wreath, be sure to make it while the vine is still green. Strip off the leaves and make a circle of several lengths, holding them securely at one end and twisting each length over the other. When you are happy with the shape, tuck in the ends and glue these in place. You can cover the join with dried flowers and herbs and perhaps a bow.

You can make your own wire shapes using thick wire (as in a coat hanger). Bend the wire into the required shape, bind it with thick twine and cover it with dried material.

Once you have decided upon the shape and style of base, choose which colors of flowers, herbs and leaves you want for the wreath. Pale pink, cream and pale blue make a lovely combination, as does a selection of gold, yellow and cream.

Decide from which point the wreath will hang and arrange your design on a symmetrical basis from that point. Insert stems into the wreath base, making sure they are secure. Glue the material into place if it does not have a stem.

Ideal plants for wreaths include yarrow, lavender, rose buds, sea lavender, goldenrod, statice, celosia, small flowers of chives, marjoram, mint and sage. Dried seed pods and berries are especially effective on country-style wreaths.

## PLANNING ARRANGEMENTS

There are few rules for creating an arrangement, but design factors must be taken into consideration.

• Where is the arrangement to sit in the room? That will dictate the size and shape.

• What colors and textures are in the immediate environment?

These factors will guide you in choosing the textures and colors of the dried flowers and plants to be used. It is always best to be guided by nature. By studying natural forms where, amazingly, everything is almost always in correct proportion, you will begin to develop an "eye" for arrangements. You will soon recognize when flowers look squashed and unsightly in the wrong-shaped container.

## CHOOSING THE RIGHT COLORS

Colors close to each other in the color spectrum mix well. As a rule, arrangements containing a mixture of red, orange, yellow and cream will look wonderful; shades of blue (statice, deep blue larkspur and sea holly); pink, cream and pale yellow (pink silene, cream statice and yellow roses); red, rust and orange (red roses, rust or orange helichrysum); or contrasting combinations of blue, yellow and green can also be successful (cornflower, yellow helichrysum and feathery acacia.)

Do not be afraid to try your own combinations, but it is usually best to choose shades of a similar intensity.

## FOLIAGE ADDITIONS

Leaves with texture are excellent as a foil to the beauty of flowers. Try to overlap each leaf slightly so that each casts a shadow on the surrounding flowers and leaves.

Each dried flower has individual beauty, so look for a range of textures through from soft, fluffy plants to those with thick, lustrous petals, and even leaves with strong veins. Each textural detail helps make the final arrangement a special achievement.

## IDEAS FOR CONTAINERS

Finding the right container is important, as is the preparation before arranging. Vases of various heights and shapes; ordinary glass containers like jars, tumblers or even a goldfish bowl; a wooden salad bowl that has outlived its use; any painted wooden box; baskets, tin buckets, old saucepans (particularly if these are copper); antique pewter mugs, and terracotta pots.

For the preparation of a basket you will need dry sphagnum moss, florist's dry foam and cellophane tape.

1 Press the dry foam into the base of basket. If necessary, cut it to shape.

2 Place a second block of dry foam, cut in the form of a small mound, on top. It ought to show about 2 inches above the basket rim.

3 Tape into position by inserting narrow tape through the basket rim and across the dry foam to slip through the cane on the other side. Cover this mound with moss.

4 Low, flat, florist's saucer-shapes are best with a dry foam block shaped to fit, stuck on a prong attached to the saucer with plastic putty. Again, cover the block with moss.

5 Most spherical vases benefit from having a loose ball of chicken wire inserted and stretched until it feels firmly in place.

6 For Christmas tree decorations, buy one of the many round dry foam shapes available from florist's suppliers; there are also cone shapes suitable for dried table arrangements. Cover these with moss, dried flower heads and herbs, place the arrangement near a color coordinating candle casting a gentle glow, and you have created a magical setting.

## HANGING UP

Whether it is a bunch of dried material, a wreath, or a swag above a fireplace, anything that hangs must have a loop from which it can be hung. It is important that the loop is hidden, so consider its design carefully. A popular way of making a loop to hang a wreath is as follows:

*Many brides like to have a keepsake of the wedding day. One of the easiest ways to do this is air-dry the bridal bouquet.*

Step Two

Try making a plaited raffia bow for a country look, as follows:

• Plait a good length of raffia strands, making the ends neat.

Step One

• Cover a piece of fairly strong stub wire with gutta-percha tape and twist a circle in the middle.

• Push the ends of the wire into the wreath base.

• Pull them back under the frame, which pulls the circle towards the frame.

• Then push each wire end into the frame on either side to secure it in position (see illustration).

Step Three

• Form a figure eight and bind this where the two ends cross over, using stub wire, leaving long ends (as on a ribbon bow).

• Attach bow to bunch with raffia twine.

*Wreaths hung on the wall are an attractive feature in any room. These are tied together with invisible thread.*

## Project One
# A GIFT BOX

Before attempting to make this attractive gift box, read through the instructions carefully and gather all the materials together. Think through the processes involved. Also think about the color combinations you prefer - this one is in cream, pink and lavender.

Have confidence in your creativity - and exercise patience. You will be pleasantly surprised at how easy this project is - and you will be delighted with the result.

MATERIALS
1 large round, square or rectangular cardboard box
1 roll of paper twist
6 ivy leaves
6 lavender heads wired into a bunch
10 nigella (love-in-a-mist) heads
6 small roses
Glue gun
Florist's scissors
Statice

*Here are some of the items you need to make this project. From left: a bunch of dried rose buds, statice, lavender, nigella, a roll of paper twist, ivy leaves, and shears.*

## METHOD

### Step One

Take the lid off the box and place it to one side. Unravel the paper twist, placing one end on the inside rim at the center of the box. Glue this into position. Bring it under the box and up to turn into the inside rim.

Cut the paper twist and glue it into position. Repeat the same steps for the lid.

### Step One

With the paper twist, cut a length of about 12 inches and unravel. Twist it around to make a rosette for the center of the box lid. Place it on the paper twist strip already in place, and glue it. That is the center of the design.

### Step Two

Place the ivy and rose leaves around each side of the rosette. Glue these into place. Position three roses on each side of the rosette and glue them.

*A selection of natural paper boxes to give you an idea of the different shapes you can create.*

## Step Three

On each side of the roses, add lavender and statice. Then add two clusters of four nigella heads, one either side of the rosette.

Make sure all stems are hidden under the central rosette, and use the glue gun carefully and sparingly.

This is a smaller box than the completed one shown on page 143, and was photographed to illustrate the question of proportion. The paper twist, ivy leaves and the first rose heads are in place. The leaves are too large for the size of box and the roses are dominating the design.

Should you wish to make a smaller box, choose small, dried material that will not take up most of the lid. Try lavender or cornflower heads and sprays of baby's breath (gypsophila).

Remember to keep a sense of proportion in each of your designs.

Project Two

# A BASKET OF PASTELS

This country-style basket of dried flowers makes the perfect gift for someone who loves a traditional interior. Set against the backdrop of a tapestry, this basket looks absolutely beautiful.

MATERIALS
1 basket made of vines
Sphagnum moss
Pale blue ribbon
Glue gun
Plastic lining
Florist's scissors
Dried camellias, rose buds, hydrangea and one dried peony

METHOD
Step One
Place the basket on a flat working surface and line it with the plastic lining. Add a thick layer of sphagnum moss over the plastic and trail strands of the moss up the handle of the basket and down to the other side.

*Opposite:*
*The completed basket of dried flowers is an attractive ornament for any room in the home. You can obviously use any flowers you like, but this is a wonderful combination so try to obtain each of these blooms to create this final effect.*

Step Two

Beginning from the left-hand side, glue five dried camellias in a row along the basket's rim, using the glue gun. Turn the basket around and do the same to the rim on the other side. When these are dry and secure, wind strands of moss around the camellias.

Step Three

On top of the bed of moss in the center of the basket, place the one dried peony. Next, add the dried hydrangea blooms, placing them slightly apart from each other around the basket. Then add the small dried rose buds and their foliage, packing them in carefully to fill any spaces.

Step Four

Tie the small blue ribbon to the handle at its base and wind it around the handle to the other side and attach the end out of sight. Lastly, carefully wind thin strands of moss through the mass of blooms.

## Project Three
# CREATING A FOCAL POINT

*Opposite:*
*The completed project is*
*magnificent on a formal*
*dining table.*

A dinner party for a celebration — be it an anniversary, Easter or
Thanksgiving — demands a memorable table centerpiece. We have designed
a colorful combination of harvest flowers, reminiscent of a country garden
planted in golden hues, for you to create for that special occasion.

If you decide to make this in a different colorway, choose a neutral candle
which does not detract from the arrangement.
For example, flowers in the pale pink and lilac ranges would suit a pale pink
candle; in the blue and purple ranges, a pale blue candle; an arrangement in
the red and orange range of the spectrum would suit a pale orange candle.
It needs to be of a reasonable height, too, but not over-powering the
arrangement, or too high in case it topples!

Arrange all of the required tools and materials on the workbench before
you start. There is nothing more frustrating than holding a fragile flower stem
in one hand, while helplessly looking for the glue gun, which is out of reach.
Work slowly and carefully, stepping back every now and then to see the
arrangement is working in a balanced way.

MATERIALS

A medium-sized cane floral ring

A piece of dry foam the size of the ring

1 thick candle in proportion to the size of the arrangement

TOOLS

Florist's wire

Glue gun

Florist's shears

FLOWERS

Golden rod

Wheat

Chinese lanterns

Oak leaves

Pinecones

Poppy heads

Seed heads of clematis

A selection of seed heads

Slices dried orange

Two bunches of cinnamon sticks, tied with pale raffia

A few dried chilli peppers

A few dried mushroom tops

## METHOD

### Step One

Tie small bunches of the seed heads together with florist's wire, ready for insertion into the dry foam at a later stage. Place these to one side. Place the cane ring on the workbench and insert the circle of dry foam into the centre. Trim until it fits perfectly. Place the dried flowers into groups.

## Step Two

Begin placing the small individual seed heads along the outer edge of the ring, pushing in the stalks firmly. When the outer edge is full, begin on the next layer, using the longer-stemmed flowers. Build up a circle of flowers until you cannot see the dry foam. Make sure you leave enough space in the center for the candle to fit neatly.

## Step Three

Once the circle of flowers is complete, wire the bunches of cinnamon sticks through the raffia tie and place into the arrangement. This is the final touch. Add the candle.

## Project Four

# TOPIARY TEMPTATION

Ideal for a breakfast setting on a special occasion, this topiary treat is also easy to construct. The number of wooden and artificial fruits will differ, depending upon which type is available in your local store. As a general rule, you will need about 10 items per tree. Do not attempt to decorate the ball before placing it in the terracotta pot securely. Step back every now and then to get a perspective on the work.

MATERIALS
1 small terracotta pot
1 block of dry florist's foam
1 round ball of dry florist's foam
Large sticks of cinnamon bark
Natural-colored reindeer moss
Artificial crab-apples
Wooden apples and pears
1 yard of orange ribbon
Glue gun
Light-gauge wire

*Opposite:*
*The topiary tree during*
*the construction phase*
*showing you the outline.*
*Next page: The completed*
*topiary trees make a*
*unique display.*

## METHOD

### Step One

To set up a topiary, spike the stem into the foam ball in the center and dribble some glue around it to make it secure. Place the block of foam into the terracotta pot and trim neatly to fit, then spike the stem into the base, also in the center, and dribble in some glue to secure it.

### Step Two

Place the bigger objects onto the topiary ball first, distributing them evenly over the ball. Glue them when you are happy with the effect. Place bits of moss in between them.

### Step Three

Cut the ribbon into smaller lengths and tie in small bows. Attach a piece of light gauge wire to the ribbon and press this into the foam ball. Make sure you have the foam ball completely covered before placing on the table.

Repeat the steps for the second topiary.

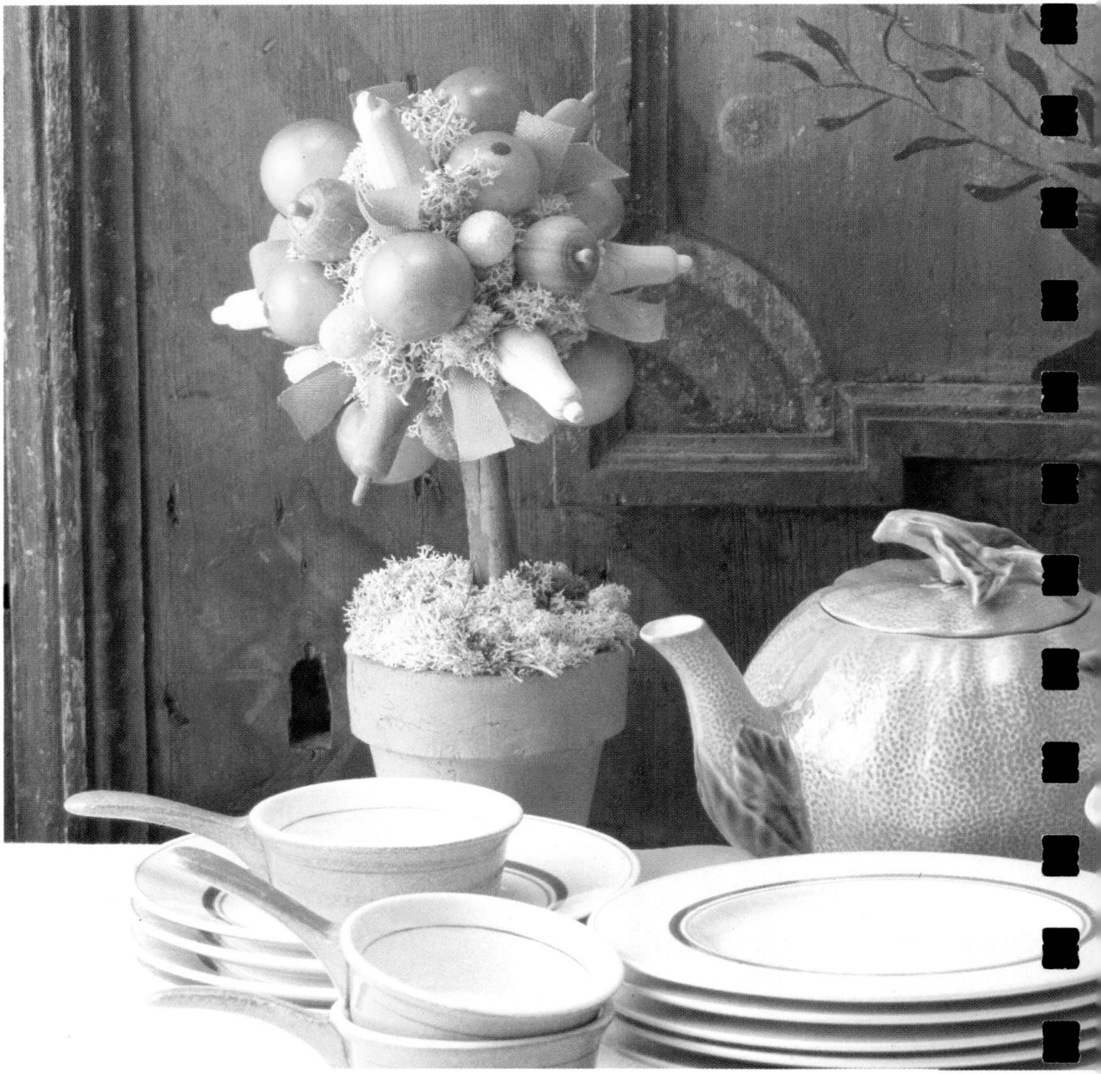

## Project Five
# DECORATED NAPKIN RINGS

*Opposite:*
*Pretty in pink and purple*
*- the completed napkin*
*rings.*

These are a super idea for a unique look for a country-style luncheon or informal dinner party. They are simple to create and will have your guests talking about the event for some time after!

  This colorway is perfect for a cream or white tablecloth. Try a deep lilac or deep pink cloth for a stronger design statement, choosing the same shade of nakpin.

MATERIALS
4 small cane napkin rings

TOOLS
Glue gun
Thin gauge florists' wire

FLOWERS
Stems of oat
Sea lavender (Latifolia)
Rose buds
Lavender 'Hidcote'
Deep pink bistort 'Elfini'
Pale mauve statice

METHOD
Step One
Place the four napkin rings on the work surface. Place each flower in a group, ready for use.

Step Two
Place a dab of glue every few inches around the napkin ring and thread the oats into the cane, pressing them firmly into place on the glued spots.

Step Three
Make five to six bunches of flowers, using one from each group selected,
and wire them together. Working in one direction around the circle, overlay
the wired bunches on the cane ring, making sure each new bunch hides the
neat stems of the previous one. Do this carefully as the flowers are fragile.
Glue in place.

## Project Six
# A COUNTRY STYLE ROSE POTPOURRI

*Opposite:*
*The final mixture*
*in a superb bowl.*

Consider the beauty of the fresh rose and imagine capturing its fragrance for many months to come. You can do this by making this unique rose-based potpourri. Follow the simple instructions and you will have a truly lovely bowl of rose fragrance to display in your favorite room. The recipe uses rose petals for its base, with lavender, hydrangea flowers, lemon verbena, aromatic cinnamon sticks, whole cloves and spicy orange peel. Ground orris root, cinnamon and nutmeg are used as fixatives and the combination is highlighted by the addition of pure rose and lavender oils. The recipe below is enough to fill an average-size salad bowl.

MATERIALS
Large china or pottery bowl for mixing the ingredients
Smaller bowl for the dried material
1/4 cup measuring scoop for measuring all ingredients
Wooden spoon for mixing
Eye-dropper
Large plastic bag with seal
Selection cones, seed pods, and wheat to decorate

Assemble the flowers, herbs and spices, fixitives and oils together with large and small bowls for mixing. Make sure all of the flowers are completely dry.

FLOWERS

20 scoops of dried mixed rose petals

2 scoops dried lavender

1 scoop hydrangea flowers

1 scoop lemon verbena or lemon scented leaves

12 cinnamon sticks

1/2 scoop cloves

1/4 scoop orange peel, ripped into tiny pieces

FIXITIVES

1/4 scoop ground nutmeg

1/4 scoop powdered cinnamon

1/4 scoop orris ground root

ESSENTIAL OILS

30 drops rose oil

20 drops lavender oil

METHOD
Step One - Preparing the Petal
Material
Place all dried rose petals, dried
flowers and leaves into the large
mixing bowl. Make sure all of this
plant material is dry. Any moisture
will ruin the entire mixture. Add
the cinnamon sticks, cloves and
orange peel. Combine the ground
nutmeg, cinnamon and orris root
in a small mixing bowl and add
to the flowers. These help to fix
the fragrance of the potpourri
and preserve the mixture. Turn
the mixture gently, using your
hands or a wooden spoon, taking
care not to crush the more delicate
ingredients.

Step Two - Adding the Essential Oils
Add the oils drop by drop, using the eye-dropper. The oil gives the mixture its dominant perfume. Surplus oil should be kept and used to 'top up' the mixture every six months or so. Mix thoroughly but carefully.

Step Three - Curing the Mixture
Place the oiled mixture in a large plastic bag and seal airtight. Leave to cure for at least seven days. The mixture is then ready to fill your favorite display bowl.

# PRESSED FLOWERS

# PREPARING TO PRESS

The craft of pressing flowers requires patience and a creative eye. From simple decorated notepaper to large framed compositions of pressed blooms, this is a craft which preserves the beauty of one of nature's most transient delights - the flower.

The craft is based on a simple concept; fresh flowers are collected and are then pressed between sheets of paper so that their moisture is absorbed. The dried, pressed specimens last indefinitely and in this form can be included in a variety of handicrafts.

People have always been fascinated by the perfection of the flowering plant and for hundreds of years the practice of pressing flowers and leaves has been used as a way of preserving their colors and forms long after the natural blooms have faded.

Like all crafts, this one has been subjected to the whims of fashion. The Victorians, for example, had a passion for pressed flowers. At this time, the craft reached dizzying heights as people went to extraordinary lengths to create increasingly elaborate pressed flower compositions. Often, embellishments such as beads, sequins and feathers were used as decorative elements.

The contemporary approach is a return to simplicity, where the beauty of the blooms is the feature. As with most cottage crafts, the simplicity of the finished article is part of its appeal.

Remember when starting off that while pressing flowers and leaves is an excellent way to preserve them, their colors and shapes are altered in the process.

A pressed flower no longer has three dimensions. It is flat and therefore two-dimensional. The pressing process alters colors significantly, sometimes intensifying, sometimes reducing them. Some pressed flowers change color altogether, while in others, aspects such as a colored center are revealed.

A pressed bloom will never be exactly the same as its fresh counterpart and an understanding of this within the framework of the craft is crucial.

*Flowers become two-dimensional and some change color during the pressing process. Compare the color of the pressed larkspur (right) with the fresh specimen. Remember this when planning pictures.*

Before attempting work on a composition or craft project, it is a good idea to spend several hours collecting and pressing various specimens and observing the results. Trial and error is an important part of the learning process and, if you are hoping to create a certain look with your work, you will be able to make the best selections from the start and avoid disappointment.

Since pressing flowers is a craft which requires careful attention to detail, clear a space in which to set out your equipment where you can work uninterrupted. You will need good light. Daylight is best. If it is not possible to work near a window, a small desk lamp with direct downlight will help. Good ventilation is important. Any hint of dampness can lead to mildew, which destroys pressed plant material.

*The herbaceous border is in full bloom, with lavatera 'Barnsley', alchillea and alchemilla mollis. Flowers beds like this are a treasure trove for pressed flower specimens.*

# ESSENTIAL EQUIPMENT

*Opposite:*
*This wire mesh tray,*
*turned upside down,*
*is a great idea, as are*
*the bulldog clips, used*
*to keep the hand-made*
*paper in place while you*
*do the arrangement.*

The essential piece is a flower press and there will be a little more detail on this later in this section. Other equipment needed includes a selection of craft and stationery items, all of which are inexpensive.

Forceps and/or tweezers are vital for handling the blooms. Tweezers with a blunt edge help avoid the risk of piercing or damaging blooms and backgrounds while arranging pressed specimens for a composition. Forceps or sharp tweezers make handling a little easier but using these require extra care until you become adept.

A magnifying glass is particularly useful when dealing with tiny elements such as seed heads or small, delicate flowers. You will also need orange (manicure) sticks or toothpicks for applying glue to the flowers.

It is a good idea to buy blotting paper for the flower press in bulk so that you always have plenty on hand. Layers of newspapers can be used as well, and household tissues are absorbent and useful as an extra layer in the press. They are also invaluable when cleaning away excess glue or fragments of dust or dried plant material.

A scalpel or craft knife is useful and can be bought from a craft store or artists' suppliers.

A small sponge, a compass and templates for drawing specific shapes are optional.

It is always a nice idea to sign your composition and a very fine marker pen is best for this. Some works, such as samplers or country herbals, require labeling or plant identification and, again, the finest of pens is the best tool. Colored inks can be used but darker colors are more easily read.

If you want to draw a border around your picture, a thicker pen will provide the best results.

A range of colorful cards
and papers to use as
backing and as mounts
for your pressed flower
works.

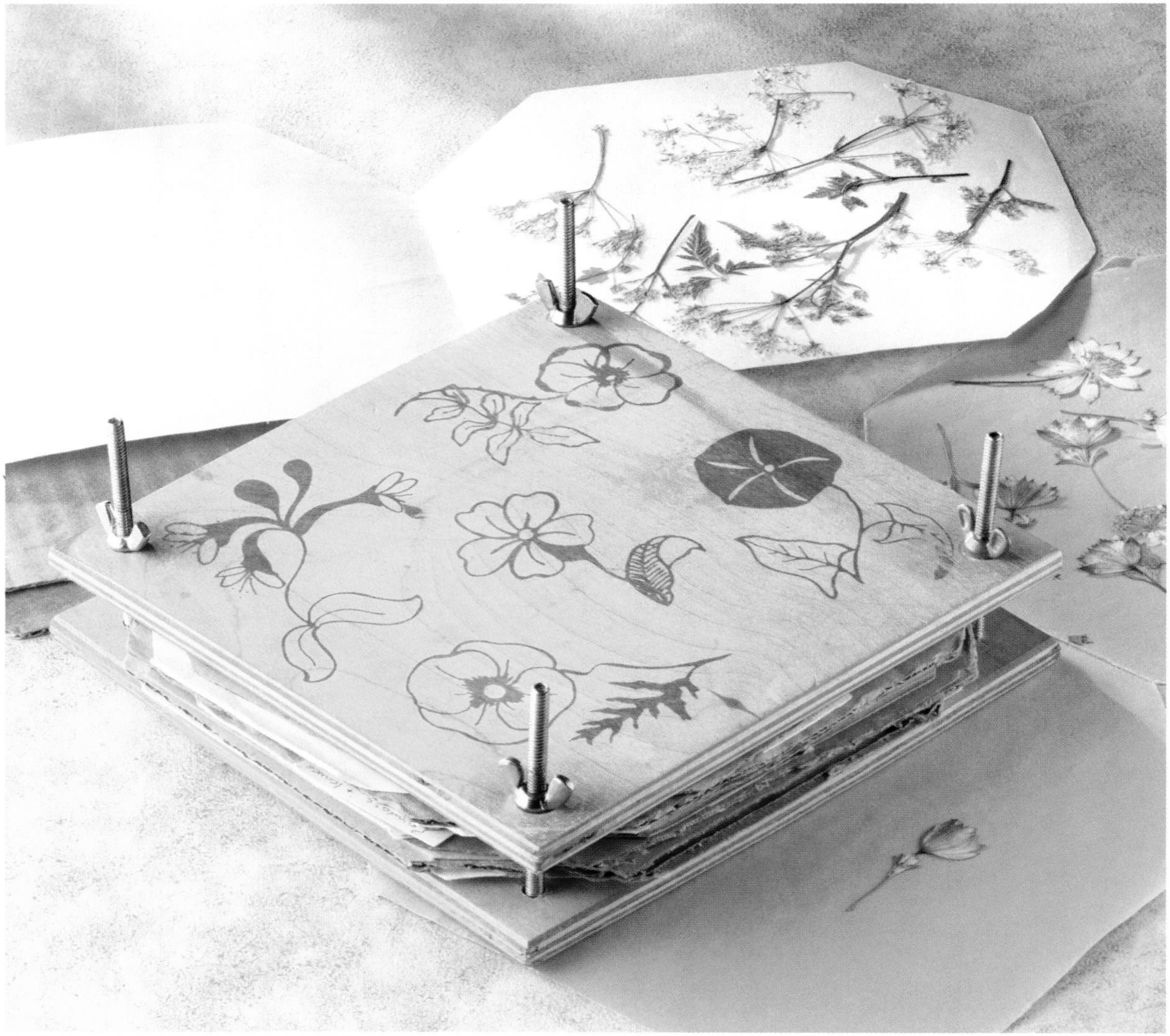

## ESSENTIALS

Flower press
Background paper
Tweezers and/or forceps
Rubber-based glue
Clear craft glue
Ruler, No. 2 pencil, eraser
Small paintbrush
Scissors, large and small
Scalpel or craft knife
Magnifying glass
Orange (manicure) sticks
Blotting paper
Masking tape
Fine marker pen

## OTHER MATERIALS

Newspaper
Tissues
Sponge
Compass
Manila envelopes
Florist's shears
Templates
Background papers

The type of work you plan to do will determine the materials needed. If you plan to decorate stationery, for example, then you will need to get in stocks of good quality paper and posterboard. Recycled papers are becoming more widely available and are an excellent idea, helping to create a slightly rustic look as well as being environmentally sound.

If you plan to create compositions of pressed flowers for framing you will need to consider background papers seriously. There are many types of paper and posterboard available and your choice will have an important bearing on the finished item.

Artists' suppliers are the best source for backing paper, but you may have to look further for specialty or unusual papers. Craft suppliers usually carry stocks of papers too.

Papers vary not only in color and texture but in weight. Generally, heavier posterboard or paper is best for large compositions and larger specimens. Lighter weight papers are fine for less elaborate compositions.

Various types of fabric can be used as a background as well. Black velvet is a favorite, as are damask and linens. Remember that creating pressed flower pictures on fabric backgrounds requires a little more care, since the fabric will be inclined to move or wrinkle more than

*Opposite:*
*This is a good example*
*of a typical flower press.*
*The top and bottom are*
*made of wood; the layers*
*are of ridged cardboard*
*and blotting paper.*
*The pressure is applied*
*by tightening the metals*
*screws at each corner.*

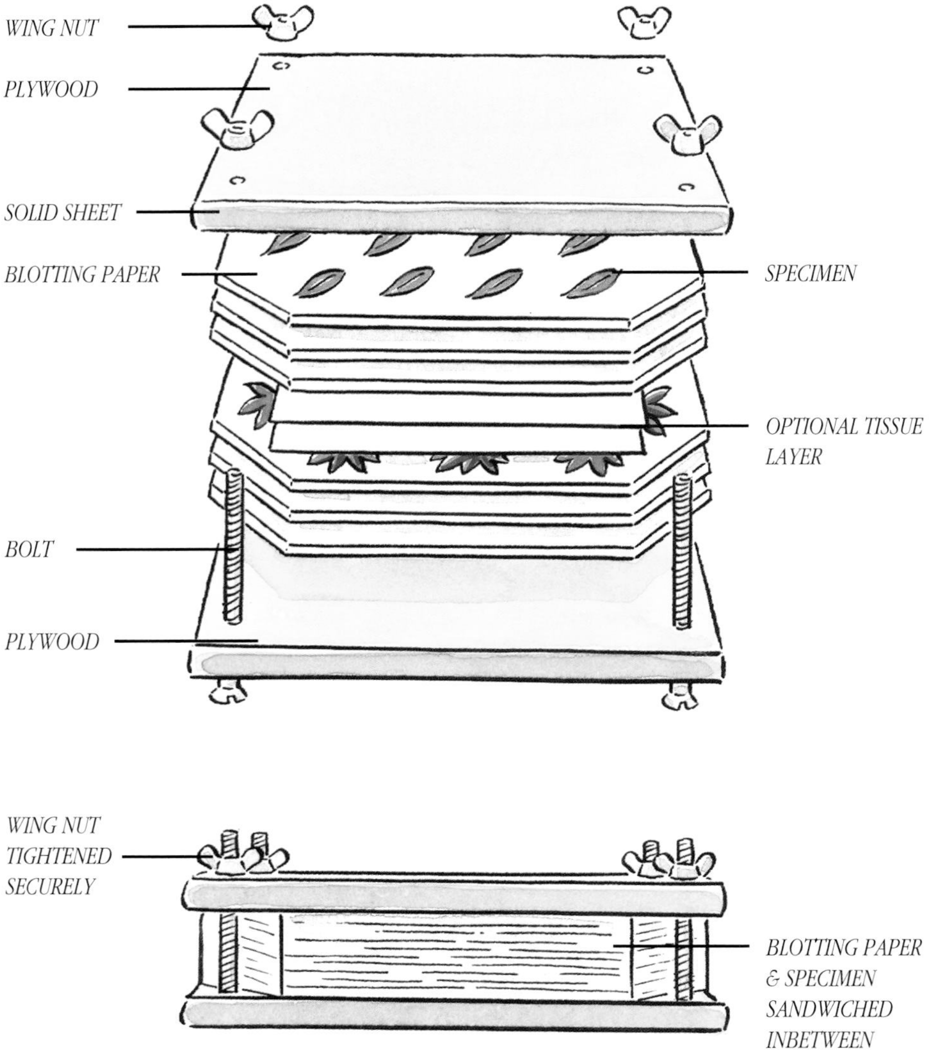

WING NUT

PLYWOOD

SOLID SHEET

BLOTTING PAPER

SPECIMEN

OPTIONAL TISSUE
LAYER

BOLT

PLYWOOD

The composition of
a basic flower press
showing the various
layers required for
correct loading (top)
and the fully loaded
press in the closed
position (below).

WING NUT
TIGHTENED
SECURELY

BLOTTING PAPER
& SPECIMEN
SANDWICHED
INBETWEEN

paper or posterboard and will probably need to be stretched slightly when framed.

## FLOWER PRESSES

The flower press is your most important piece of equipment and, if you plan to get involved in the craft on a regular basis, it is worth buying or making one.

At the beginning you can improvise by pressing blooms between the pages of a book weighted with heavy objects, or using two pieces of plywood and several bricks as a temporary press. A good basic press, however, will help make your work more professional and more pleasurable.

A basic flower press is comprised of two pieces of plywood cut into a rectangular shape. The plywood should be of a reasonably heavy gauge to withstand wear and tear. The pieces are joined with six bolts and wing nuts, one at each corner and two on either side.

To operate the press, the wing nuts are removed, the top piece of plywood taken off and the press loaded with specimens, carefully arranged between layers of blotting paper. When the press is full, the top piece of plywood is replaced and the wingnuts screwed into place and gradually tightened over a period of time to exert sufficient pressure to press the flowers sandwiched in between.

If you do not have the facilities for making your own, flower presses are available from craft suppliers and some specialty stores. If you eventually take up the craft in a serious way, you can invest in a professional flower press which works by means of a central screw mechanism. These are much bigger and easier to operate than the type of press we have described here and will enable you to press a greater variety of plant material more quickly.

When your press is not in use, make sure it is completely cleared of all fragments of plant material and stored, with the wing nuts loosened, in a well-ventilated place. A good circulation of air prevents dampness which can lead to the growth of mildew and fungi.

## PICTURE FRAMES

If you are planning to create pressed flower pictures, they will require framing to show them to their best advantage. Professional framing for a lot of pressed flower pictures could prove a costly exercise, so it is worth considering a do-it-yourself approach.

*A superb range of pre-cut frames is available to complete your pressed flower picture.*
*This selection includes country-style wood and laminated, as well as marbled, frames.*

There are a number of options. The easiest method involves purchasing a do-it-yourself framing kit such as those available from specialty framers and some hardware stores. Photo frames from photographic suppliers are another possibility. Or you can buy ready made lengths of frame and cut them to your own specifications.

Glass is essential to protect the delicate plant material. Non-reflective glass will help cut down on the ultra-violet rays which hasten fading, but may result in loss of picture detail.

The mount you choose helps center a work, separating it from the frame and drawing the eyes to the detail and color of the composition.

Because plants - even pressed flowers - are bulky compared to a print or painting, the frame must be deep enough to accommodate this. A professional framer will make the appropriate allowance, and you must, too. A small piece of plywood placed at each corner of the mount before the frame is added should prove adequate.

*Lace is ideal for using either as the only mount on delicate pictures, or as an additional decorative element. Make sure you choose the right width of lace, A strip too thin will look lost.*

# HINTS FOR SUCCESS

Collecting your own plant material is one of the most delightful elements of this craft. You can gather flowers from your own yard or elsewhere, or even plan a special expedition to the countryside to pick wildflowers. City-dwellers do not have to be limited to making selections from their local florist - although this provides a wealth of seasonal material. Even a balcony garden or windowsill herb garden can provide sufficient material for a small-scale project.

If you are limited to purchasing your plant material rather than gathering it, try to go to the source of supply - the flower markets. In most areas these are held early in the morning. The range of flowers is large and you may be able to buy leftover bunches at reduced prices at the end of a morning's trading.

Plants and flowers are at their best in the morning so pick them after the early morning dew has dried. Seasonal blooms should be gathered early in the season rather than at the end of their flowering cycle.

Bear conservation in mind when you gather raw materials to press. Take only as much as you need, as you would from your own yard. Do not pick blooms and leaves indiscriminately and be most careful to leave buds and shoots intact.

Botanical gardens and national parks are strictly out of bounds as they contain many protected species. In some parks and gardens you may be prohibited from removing fallen blooms, too. It is always wise to check before taking anything from these areas. Many wildflowers and native plants are grown commercially and are available through florists when in season.

As your skills progress, so too will your knowledge of what to pick. Initially, it is a good idea to gather a wide variety of plant material - leaves, flowers, sprays, as well as individual blooms, seed heads, flowers with stems intact, grasses and even weeds. Charming compositions can be created from plants commonly thought of as weeds - dandelions, common daisies and buttercups for example, or ferns and ivy. All of these can be pressed successfully.

| Color | Effect |
|---|---|
| WHITE | tends to become off-white or cream |
| BLUES | tend to become deeper |
| PINKS | tend to fade to a lighter shade |
| GREENS | tend to be subject to most variation |
| REDS | tend to become more intense |
| YELLOWS | tend to become a shade darker |
| ORANGES | tend to look brighter |

When selecting leaves and flowers for the press, make sure they are as near to perfect as possible. Flowers should be undamaged and without any browning on the edges of the petals.

All insect life must be removed from the plant. Check carefully on the undersides of leaves and inside flowers (as much as you can without damaging the bloom) for any signs of life. Some tiny species may escape your notice at first glance but it is essential to locate them and remove them. If they are left, insects which feed on flowers can continue to do so during the early stages of pressing and blooms may emerge damaged.

Flowers should be pressed as soon as possible after picking. If you are out in the country, place your plant material in a plastic bag, taking care not to overfill it. If you can, separate specimens into some sort of order as you go - herbs in one bag, leaves in another, buds in another, and so on. Some air in the bag will help protect the plants. If, on arriving home, the blooms appear to have wilted, place the bag in the refrigerator for an hour or two to help them revive.

*Here is another example
of how color changes
during the pressing
process. This kangaroo's
paw turns from a fresh
yellow to brown*

A basic botanical knowledge of the flowering plant will prove a useful asset to this craft and there are any number of books on the subject. A general understanding of the growing cycles of various plants will help you know when is the best time of year to gather or buy specimens, while a knowledge of the structure of the flower itself will help when it comes to specific pressing techniques such as pulling flowers apart and "reconstructing" them. (This will be discussed in more detail in the next section.)

It is important to keep an open mind when gathering plants for pressing. Some of the prettiest blooms in their natural state do not press as well as some of the simple flowers.

Color changes are the most variable factor you will have to contend with. All plants will look different after pressing and, while there are no rigid rules, the following guidelines are worth remembering.

Using a bright color for the main card and a white or cream card as the background for the composition creates a more striking effect. Always ensure the pattern is centered.

*An abundance of roses
and campanulas in the
garden bed provides the
perfect source for flowers
to pick and press.*

## PLANTS FOR THE BEGINNER'S PRESS

Place plant material in the press as quickly as possible to insure good results and the best possible colors in the pressed specimen. Speed at this stage also minimizes damage to blooms.

The longevity of pressed flowers is brought about by the extraction of moisture during pressing. To achieve maximum absorption, flowers should be placed between several sheets of an absorbent material such as blotting paper or newspaper plus several layers of tissues. As the press is screwed down tight, the flowers sandwiched in between are flattened and their moisture content absorbed by the material above and below them.

To load the press, cut several sheets of blotting paper to the same size as the press. Lay three or four sheets of paper to form a base. Arrange the fresh specimens

| Flowers | Leaves | Herbs |
| --- | --- | --- |
| daisies | ivy/most species | lavender |
| larkspurs | maidenhair fern | fennel |
| roses/rose buds | asparagus fern | sweet basil |
| anemones | shield fern/fronds & leaves | marjoram |
| pansies | eucalyptus leaves | parsley |
| statice | holly, bay laurel | |
| hydrangea | maple leaves | chamomile |
| fuchsia | seeded grasses | sage |

*Lobelia and pansies pressed on one sheet of blotting paper have been in the press for some weeks. They have a diary note attached, marking the date they were picked and placed in the press. The other sheet displays cow parsley.*

*Top right and far right: Arrange fresh specimens on a sheet of blotting paper and place on base layer. Place a protective layer of tissue between the specimens and the next layer of blotting paper.*

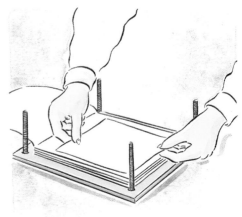

*Bottom right and far right: Keep plants in specimen groups if possible. Continue layering paper and specimens in this way until the press is full. Do not overload the press.*

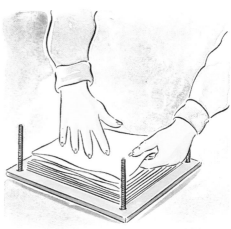

carefully on another sheet of blotting paper, allowing a little space around each one. If you wish, you can lay a protective layer of tissue over the flowers before placing another sheet of blotting paper on top. Continue in this way, layering flowers and paper, until the press is full. Do not overload the press.

It is a good idea to keep plants in groups if you can; a sheet of daisies, for example, or a sheet of ivy leaves. This not only insures even pressure in the press but reduces handling of the specimens after pressing and makes their storage easier.

Once the press is loaded, screw it down as tightly as possible. As the bulk reduces during the following days, continue tightening the press by screwing down the wing nuts or increasing the amount of weight on top.

Bulkier plants require more pressure than delicate ones. Ideally, the two should not be placed side by side on the same sheet of paper as this can result in uneven pressure and an unsatisfactory result.

Flowers should be left in the press for six weeks. You can check their progress every now and then — the relative dampness of the blotting paper will give you some indication of how things are going - but it is recommended that you leave all specimens for at least six weeks.

Some experts advise changing the top sheet of absorbent paper regularly throughout the pressing process. Others feel this is unnecessary except in the case of particularly moist plant material such as succulents. Again, trial and error is your best guide.

For beginners, try changing the paper every few days at first, taking care not to dislodge the blooms. Work out your own rules as you become familiar with the procedure.

Once satisfied that the flowers are well pressed, you must also be quite sure they are completely dry before taking them out of the press. Specimens should be gently loosened from the sheet of blotting paper before being stored.

## STORING SPECIMENS
You will need some sort of storage system for your pressed specimens. A flat, plastic stacking unit such as those available from most stationery stores is deal, but a series of large manila envelopes kept flat in a carton will do just as well. Take care to label envelopes or sheets accurately, not forgetting to add the date.

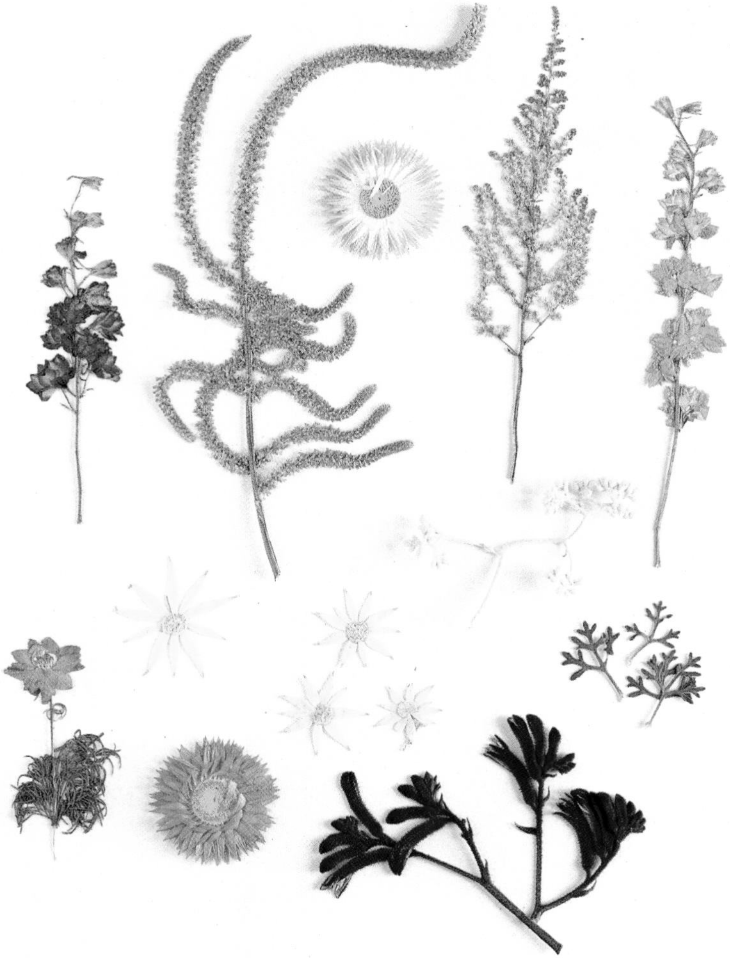

*This selection of pressed
flowers shows the various
characteristics of eleven
species.*

One of the cardinal rules of this craft is never to throw anything away. Even parts of a plant which have been damaged in the press, or broken apart during handling, may eventually find a place in a future composition. For the same reason, it is a good idea to press all the parts of a plant. Rather than separating the flower and discarding the leaves, stems and buds, press these too and store them for possible use later on.

Always press more than you think you are going to need. Even if a single bloom is all you require for a project, press several so that you have some in reserve in case the specimen gets damaged during handling. This is particularly important for plants which have a very short flowering season. If you are working on a composition based on spring-flowering bulbs, for example, and run out of flowers, you will have to wait an entire year before being able to supplement the material.

## SPECIAL TECHNIQUES

While in most cases, flowers, leaves and grasses are loaded into the press as you see them, there are some plants which will not press successfully because of their bulk or shape. In cases such as these,

specimens can be pulled apart, the various parts pressed individually and the flower "reconstructed" after pressing. Plants can also be cut into two sections which are placed together again after pressing, or you may find that the cross-section reveals an interesting center which can add another dimension to your work.

*A selection of simple cottage garden plants in cream and yellow has been used to fashion this heart. Lightly pencil in the outline on the background paper and place the largest blooms in position first.*

*Right:*
*If bulky plant material proves difficult to press, trim away excess parts such as the lower end of the stalk using sharp scissors.*

*Far right:*
*Fleshy flowers such as the hyacinth can be cut in half and then pressed. Use a scalpel to ensure the bloom is cut cleanly. Once pressed the two halves can be used individually or placed together to form a complete flower.*

*Bottom:*
*Flowers which prove difficult to press because of their size can be carefully pulled apart, the various parts pressed separately, then reconstructed.*

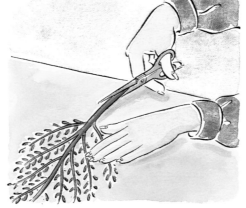

The use of cross-sections is a deliberate device employed by many pressed flower artists, as is the use of individual petals, stems and even the smaller parts of the flower such as the stamen.

Another device you can use to create a different effect is to press flowers that are closed or partly open by carefully laying some petals back and others forward. This works very well if you are using several blooms from the same species, as it allows you to capture the full range of the plant's flowering cycle.

Tricks such as this can be used for damaged specimens too. Petals can be replaced using a touch of glue, a broken

*The name is made from pressed plant material, framed to last through the years. This is a great idea as a gift to a new-born child. It is something they will have to treasure forever.*

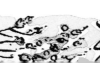

*An example of the imaginative use of pressed flowers is seen here in the small cameo and small circular ash tray. The flowers are violas and heartsease.*

stem can be repaired in the same way and in some instances, where leaves, stems and blooms have been pressed separately, it is possible to reconstruct the entire plant.

Color enhancement is another useful technique. While in most cases a flower's natural color (even those which change or fade in the press) is the most desirable, there are instances where color can be boosted for an effect. Certain plants are renowned for color loss after pressing; lavender is one, freesias are another.

The most effective way to add color to pressed flowers is with spray-on color and specialty florist's spray color packs are available in a wide range of hues. Used sparingly, color enhancers can add depth to a composition. Too much will give your work an unnatural look. You will soon learn which flowers respond to the addition of color and which are best left *au naturel.*

*Framed pressed flower pictures can bring a touch of the garden to any room in the house. This pretty scene is on top of a dressing table.*

Ferns and pansies feature strongly in this collection of items made using pressed flowers. They are easy to make and ideal as gifts for friends and family.

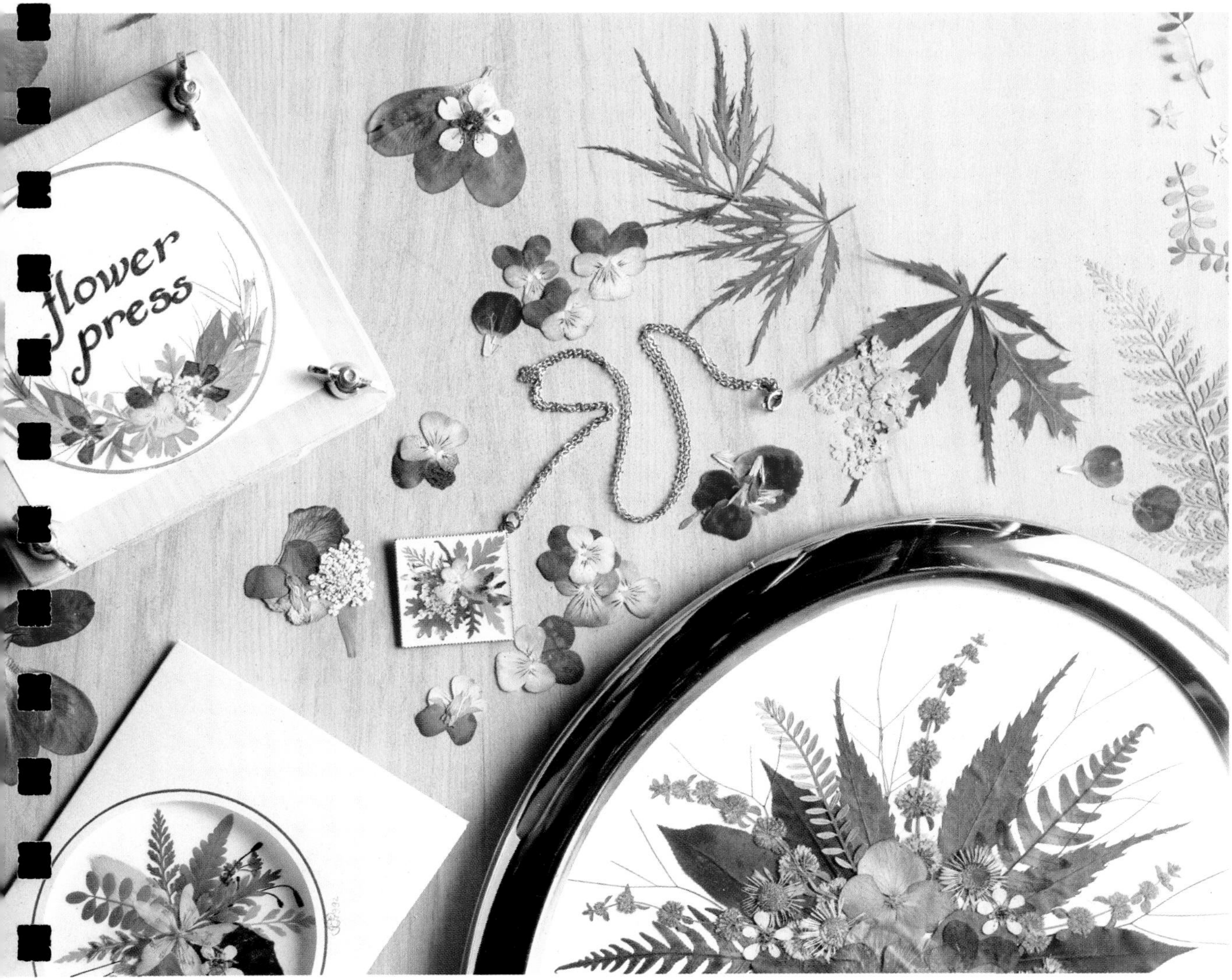
flower
press

# DESIGN CONSIDERATIONS

Using the flowers you have pressed in a project is the ultimate objective of this craft and there are many attractive projects from which to choose. The traditional ones include pressed flower pictures, which can take on many forms; pressed flower stationery, where simple combinations of pressed specimens are used to decorate notepaper and cards; and pressed flower decorations, where blooms are used to embellish items such as photograph frames, little storage boxes and so on.

While quite different from one another, all of these projects rely on your own creativity and it is this stage which is the most satisfying and enjoyable.

There are basic pointers relating to composition which can be followed, but your own interpretation of color, form and style will prove most important to the finished work.

## SIX ESSENTIALS FOR COMPOSITION

Balance
Shape
Color
Mood
Texture
Style

## BALANCE

The best way to arrange an attractive composition is to move your selection of blooms carefully around until you achieve a pattern that pleases you and appears balanced. The easiest way to do this is to create a focal point using a central bloom. Select a relatively large specimen for the focal point and, from here, work up and out using either curves, straight lines or any similar device which helps create the feeling of movement. Your aim is to take the eye from the center of the composition outwards to embrace the whole.

*A pressed flower circlet makes a delightful composition. Use a compass to draw a perfect circle lightly onto your background paper and let a little of the background show through between the flowers to give the composition a lighter feeling.*

Note: Turning an arrangement upside down is a useful trick to check the balance of a composition.

## COLOR

This is the essence of most art forms and it is the most important element in creating impact. The primary colors of red, yellow and blue are the brightest in the spectrum. Used together they create impressions that are cheerful, dramatic and vibrant.

Secondary colors such as green, violet and pink are softer. Used together they convey an impression that is soft and romantic. Black and white are used for contrast and the darker colors such as browns and grays help create mood within a group of brighter hues. You will find that the softer colors harmonize more easily with one another than the stronger colors and beginners may find it easier to work on a project based on one color group at first.

If pressed specimens have been stored according to their color, this will make your task a lot easier. As you become more familiar with the way various colors work together you can experiment with more unusual combinations.

## TEXTURE

Since pressed flowers have been reduced to two-dimensional objects, the element of texture takes on a special importance.

By using different textures in a composition, you add visual interest and help add dimension and a sense of scale. Pressed flowers with a smooth or even texture are possibly the commonest and usually form the basis of a composition.

Specimens such as seeded grasses, spiky leaves and taller flowers can be used to add a coarser texture and provide vertical lift, while seed heads, sprays of plants such as baby's breath and spreading fern fronds provide softness and an impression of horizontal movement.

## SHAPE

Since you will be working with a variety of shapes, great care must be taken in the placement of blooms to achieve an overall shape which does not overwhelm the eye. As a starting point, it is a good idea to follow the shapes florists use when working with fresh flowers, such as posies, bouquets, wreaths and garlands. By tradition, these shapes work to show the blooms off to best advantage so it makes sense to follow similar principles when working with pressed flowers.

As you develop your own style you may wish to deviate from traditional ideas but, for the beginner, a posy of pressed flower blooms following a color theme on a plain background paper makes a charming project. Contrary to expectations, the simplest shapes present a higher degree of difficulty to arrange than more crowded compositions. The latter allows room for error, whereas arrangements featuring individual plants need to be perfect in every detail.

*A long and thin stem like this larkspur dictates the shape of any composition in which it may be used. It might be best to use it on its own, with a lace mount, and a pretty frame. You could create a series of shapes and hang them along one wall space.*

*Next page:*
*A child's name in flowers. This delightful idea was created for a baby's nursery and the flowers include forget-me-nots and miniature rose buds. Make sure you have a wide selection of pressed material to hand before beginning a composition like this.*

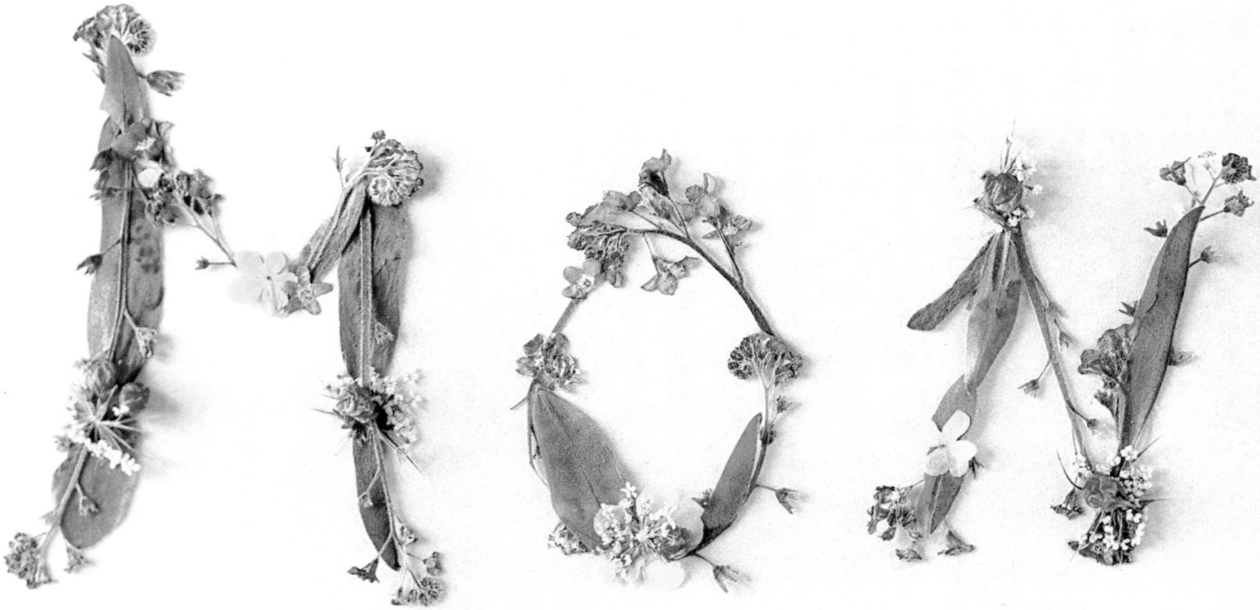
MOM

MOOD

As color is one of the most crucial elements when considering the mood of a pressed flower project, first select your color theme, such as pink, blue or gold, then work to create a mood with those colors. Yellow, for example, combined with clear green and a little red or blue will create a cheerful and bright composition. However, combined with pastel colors, white and soft greens, the effect is different. Remember that the background you choose will have a profound effect on the mood of your project.

STYLE

This is the most difficult element to define since style is an interpretation of your own creativity. However, as you progress with the craft, you will soon develop a style that is recognizable. Your choice of colors, blooms and themes will result in a unique composition. There are a number of recognized styles which you can aim for initially. Some of the most popular include the country look, in which simplicity of color and form achieves a naive charm; the romantic look, in which soft pastel colors and pretty combinations of shapes create feminine appeal; the natural look, in which wild flowers are arranged the way that they appear in nature; and finally, the lush and exotic look, which defies convention (and nature) with its completely individual combinations of colors and blooms.

# TECHNIQUES OF THE CRAFT

Once you have decided on a composition, you must then arrange it on the chosen background and secure it in place. Make sure you have all the necessary equipment on hand. Take all possible precautions to avoid interruptions.

Place a quantity of glue in a shallow dish so it is easy to use. Rubber-based glue is good as it does not dry as quickly as clear glue. Then, using tweezers or forceps, carefully lift each bloom. Use an orange (manicure) stick to dab a small amount of glue on the center of the underside, choosing the stalk, stem, or strongest part of the plant. Avoid placing glue in the middle of delicate petals where it may show through; work with the center of the tip instead.

Continue to lift each specimen in turn, applying glue and replacing the flower carefully on the background. You may find it useful to apply a thin layer of rubber-based glue to the background paper itself in the shape of your arrangement.

Using scissors, trim any excess pieces of stalk or leaf. With a small brush, remove excess bits and pieces of plant material. Excess glue should be removed immediately. Too much glue can dry to a shiny blob on your work.

Fixing your arrangement in place requires care and patience more than any particular skill. The procedure will be time consuming at first, but as you become more adept at handling the pressed specimens, you will gradually become faster.

Once you have fixed all the plant material in place, allow the composition plenty of time to dry. Store it carefully, away from drafts, in a warm, dry place, out of any direct sunlight. Once a pressed flower picture is thoroughly dry (test it by moving the whole piece very gingerly,) it is ready to be framed.

Note: The finished composition will be quite dry, very brittle and easily damaged, so take care when storing the work or transporting it to the framer.

*Following pages:*
*A profusion of brightly colored pressed flowers makes a cheerful picture to hang on a wall.*

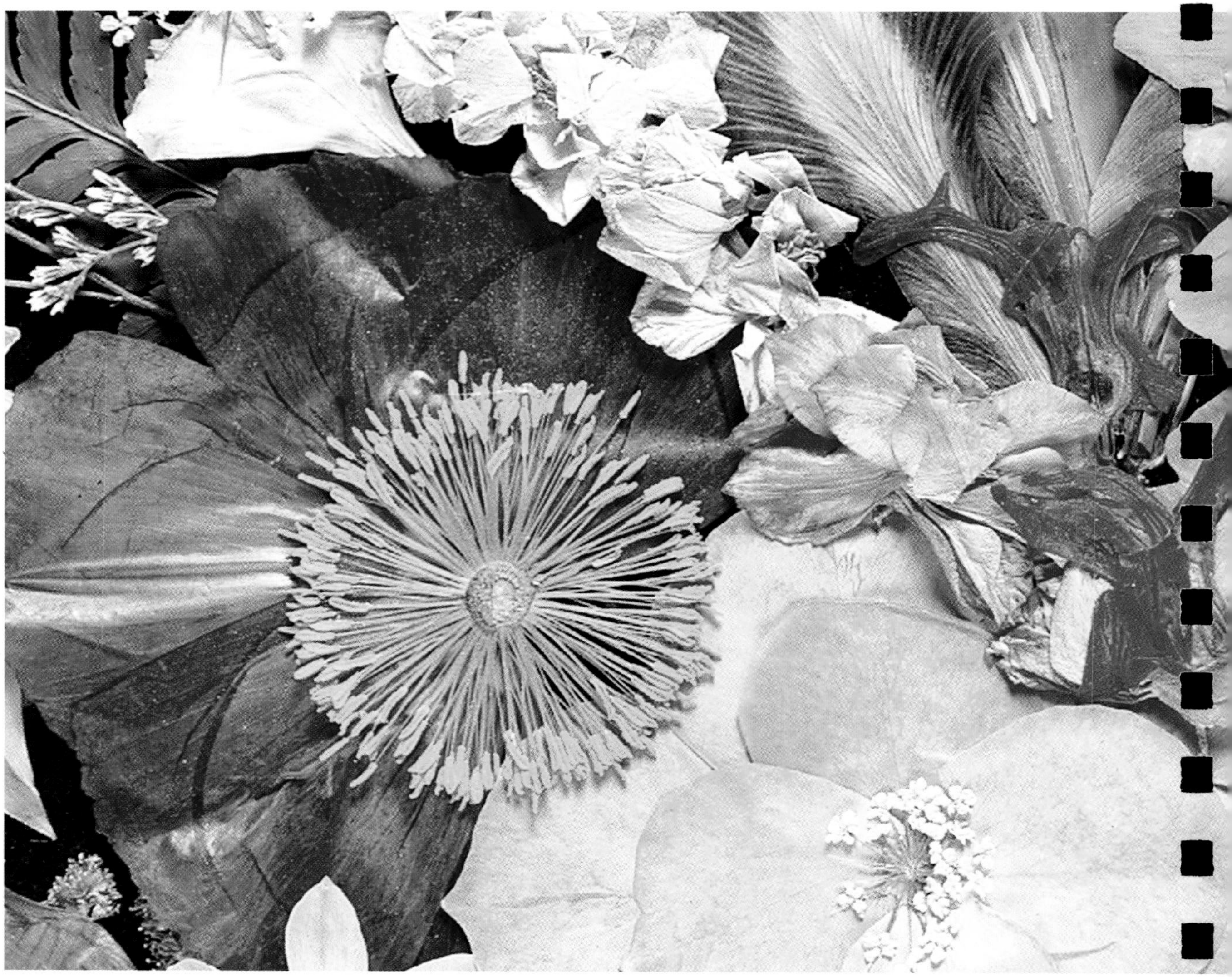

*Right:*
Move the pressed flowers around on the background until you are happy with their position.

*Far right:*
Fix the larger specimens in place first.

*Right:*
Use a cocktail stick to apply glue to center underside of the flower.

*Far right:*
Replace the flower on the background taking care not to smudge glue.

*Above left:*
*Trim away excess plant material from the edges of the picture.*

*Above:*
*Use tweezers or forceps to move the smaller blooms into position.*

# FINISHING TOUCHES

The most popular of all pressed flower projects are pressed flower pictures. The range of possibilities is infinite and may eventually surpass the hanging space on your walls. Pictures can be of any size, from miniatures to large collages, creating all sorts of decorative effects.

## POSIES AND BOUQUETS

Arrangements which follow familiar floral shapes such as the posy or bouquet make an excellent starting point for a pressed flower picture. The theme can be based on color, the seasons, or you can press blooms from a special-occasion posy or wedding bouquet to turn into a souvenir pressed flower picture. You can aim for a simple effect such as a summer posy created from pressed daisies, cornflowers and baby's breath, or a luxurious bouquet featuring lilies for a more formal design.

## WREATHS AND GARLANDS

Because these have a definite form, a little more discipline is required in their creation. The look is a romantic one and calls for soft colors and a good mix of specimens, from open flowers to buds.

At the beginning, it will help if you draw the outline of your shape in pencil on the background paper. Use a compass to draw the circular outline required for a wreath. As a finishing touch, you can add a bow of narrow, satin ribbon to the completed picture.

Be precise in the arrangement of the blooms and aim to let a little of the background material show through between the flowers to prevent the picture from becoming too heavy. Specimens which have a natural curve will work to your advantage and each bloom should be carefully positioned with the finished shape in mind.

## HERBALS AND SAMPLERS

Herbals and botanical compositions are based on the traditional lists and drawings used by herbalists and botanists thousands of years ago. Their simple form is appealing. Some botanical compositions rely on a single plant meticulously reconstructed and labeled. Others require a series of plants which are arranged in ordered rows. Simple plants are the best choice. Garden herbs, wild flowers, or "cottage garden" species can all be used effectively.

It is a good idea to press at least three of the individual specimens you plan to use, that way you will be assured of a margin for error. When working with a series of plants such as you might find in a true herbal, keep a careful eye on the balance of your composition and take care not to let any one specimen dominate the picture.

If the plants are to be labeled, make sure there is enough room on the background paper. A floral sampler imitates its cross-stitch counterpart. It can be composed on a seasonal theme - a spring sampler for example - or as a personal record of your own favorite flowers. Again, this formalized type of composition offers a special challenge and you will need to be exact in selecting flowers for size and scale as well as color and form. When working with a single specimen plant, select small, compact species for best results.

## BASKETS AND COLLAGES

The starting point for a basket composition is the basket itself.

There are several ways of doing this: one is to cut out a basket shape from a material such as flat woven cane which can be bought by the yard. Use a pattern cut from heavy posterboard for the outline and attach it securely to the background paper.

Another method is to create a basket from dried grasses, woven together, then glued and cut to shape. A similar effect can be achieved using pressed fern fronds carefully glued onto posterboard cut into a basket shape.

You could use brown or green poster-card or fabric beneath your "basket" for a more realistic effect. Once in place, work from the top of the basket and arrange your pressed flowers to form the outline of the finished shape, then fill in the center.

A pressed flower collage is the least disciplined of all the pictorial compositions. Themes can be inspired by color, the time of year, your own property, or perhaps the forest. A collage can be dramatic, romantic, simplistic or luxuriant. Try various combinations of color and texture, mix unusual shapes and sizes and add obscure or rare species for an exotic effect.

The element of dimension is an interesting one to experiment with. Try placing tall, spiky blooms in the foreground, fading to a distant mass of smaller flowers behind. Non-plant material can be added for an individual look: tiny beads, feathers, little sea shells and ribbon all work well.

## PRESSED FLOWER DECORATION

Side tables and jewelry boxes and many other items can be decorated in this way. For the beginner, smaller objects such as little papier-mâché boxes or a wooden photograph frame, make pleasing projects. First insure the surface of the item to be decorated is smooth. If necessary, sand it lightly with fine-grained sandpaper. Select the flattest pressed material, arrange it and secure in place using craft glue.

To protect the surface, several coats of clear varnish should be applied. As this can alter the colors of some pressed flowers, experiment with blooms and varnish on a sheet of paper before starting work.

## PRESSED FLOWER STATIONERY

Using pressed flowers to personalize greeting cards and notepaper is a delightful idea and it is always appreciated by the recipient. You can purchase blank cards and heavyweight notepaper, or you can make your own.

First, cut the card to the required size. With the card flat, carefully make an arrangement of pressed blooms and glue these into place. Protect the work with a sheet of blotting paper and place a flat weight such as book on top until glue has dried thoroughly. There are any number of ideas for decorating stationery; single specimens are simple to work with on this small scale, or you could make a series of cards all featuring the same plant or arrangement.

Tiny posies and wreaths can be added to the center of a card, or a single rosebud and leaf in the top corner of notepaper creates a charming effect. Add a finely

*Personalize your own stationery by decorating it with pressed flowers. Here a selection of small-scale blooms has been used to create attractive and distinctive notepaper.*

drawn border and hand-lettering, or create a cameo shape by arranging the blooms on an oval of fabric which has been glued to the center of the card.

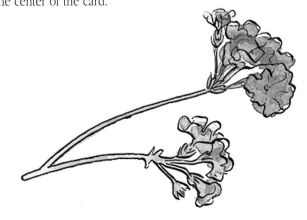

## Project One

# A COUNTRY-STYLE HERBAL

This delightful, country-style herbal makes an ideal beginner's project.
It is based on a combination of familiar pressed flowers and garden herbs.
The nine pressed herbs have been labeled and then "framed" within a border
of pressed flowers and leaves based on a color scheme of cream and green.
Handmade paper has been used for the background and the finished
composition has been framed with a simple timber frame without a mount.

MATERIALS
**You will need:**
1 piece handmade or similar paper 16 x 20 inches
1 piece lightweight posterboard 16 x 20 inches
Plain timber frame cut to fit.

**Pressed Plant Material:**
9 different herbs:
Italian parsley and curly-leaf parsley, oregano, rosemary, caraway, sage,
thyme, marjoram and mint.
8 different cream/green flowers and leaves:
Queen Anne's Lace (wild carrot), guelder-rose, astilbe, white larkspur,
thryptomene, verbascum, hydrangea, forget-me-not and plain and variegated
ivy leaves.

*The simple form of a traditional herbal such as might have been created by botanists and herbalists thousands of years ago, has a perennial charm. Follow the instructions carefully and yours, too, will look like this.*

*Step One
Create the floral
border first.*

Note: The choice of herbs and flowers may be varied according to availability or individual preference.

Step One
Glue the background paper to the posterboard. Allow to dry.

Form a border right around the edge of the paper approximately 1 1/2 inches wide using the Queen Anne's Lace laid on its side as shown overleaf .

Glue in place.

Make the edge neat by trimming excess plant material with scissors.

Step Two
Fill in the border by adding layers of the other flowers and ivy leaves.

Place the largest specimens first and fill in any gaps with the smaller flowers.

Place the smallest flowers, the forget-me-nots, last. Glue in place.

Step Three
Arrange the pressed herbs in three rows of three in the following order:

row 1   oregano
        rosemary
        Italian parsley
row 2   caraway
        sage
        curly-leaf parsley
row 3   thyme
        marjoram
        mint

Glue in place.

Step Four
Label each of the herbs as shown, using a fine marker pen. Allow to dry and frame to suit.

The finished project in its simple frame makes an ideal picture for a country-style kitchen or informal dining room.

*Step Three*
*Arrange the pressed herbs in rows of three across and vertically.*

Project Two
# PICTURE FOR A FRIEND

This charming picture is created with a collection of pale grasses, which are mounted on a white paper background. The dark green mount and the pale pine picture frame complete the composition.

The design is loose but centered on the tall stem of oat grass.

MATERIALS
Adhesive
One tall stem of oat grass
Ferns
Grasses
White card

Step One
Cut one piece of white matt finish card to the size required.

Place the collection of grasses nearby, trim any extraneous material from the stems and place the tall grass stem in the center of the card.

*A lovely picture for a friend is made simply of pressed oat grasses. Its simplicity is the key to its success.*

Step Two

Cut the stems of the other grasses to the various lengths to suit the design. The ferns at the bottom of the design can be quite short so that they fit across the width of the center of the collection.

Place each piece on to the card and arrange them until you are happy with the way they look.

Step Three

Take each piece carefully off the card and place in the same design on the work surface. Spray the design area of the card with adhesive and, using tweezers, place each piece back in position on to the card.

Press firmly in place, using a sheet of paper between your hand (or whatever you are using the press) and the arrangement. Leave to dry. Frame.

## Project Three
# A PRETTY CARD

Here is a great idea for a friend, using the initial of their first name.
The design should take up most of the card, as shown in the project card.
You may like to use numbers instead for a birthday card, as seen in the
photograph of the card with '21' floral design.

MATERIALS
Adhesive
Pencil and fine ink pen
Ruler
White card
Selection of pressed flower petals

*The card before the addition of the main image.*

Step One
Cut the piece of white card to the
size required. Pencil in the border
lines to your own design, and go over
the pencil with the ink pen when the
lines are in the required position.
You can use any color of ink - black always looks smart, but you may
prefer to use one of the dominant colors in the selection of flower petals.

Step Two

Draw the outline of the initial in pencil. Do this carefully. Cut tiny pieces of flower petals and have them in a line handy to the card. Spray the card within the initial with adhesive, and carefully put the tiny bits of flowers in place, keeping within the outlines. When you have filled the outline, press firmly in place, using a sheet of paper between your hand (or whatever you are using to press) and the arrangement. Leave to dry.

*You may like to do a special occasion card, such as this one for a friend's 21st birthday.*

*The completed card with the recipient's initial centered on it within a fine ruled border.*

NOTE: This design has a bottom central yellow bloom focal point, and the same yellow flower has been used at the top of each of the angles of the capital 'V'. This is a small design detail but it does add to the picture and is worth following for the effect. Try to use just three or four colors, and make sure you balance each side of the V.

## Project Four

# A FLORAL TRIBUTE

Sweet violets are the theme of this lovely collection of gift cards. The floral theme is very popular with people of all ages, and the white background gives this collection a sophisticated look.

MATERIALS
Adhesive
Envelopes to fit card size
Ink pen
Pencil
Pressed violets
Selection of other small pressed flowers and leaves
Ruler
Tweezers
White card

METHOD
Step One
Draw the border of the card in pencil and when you are happy with it, go over the pencil with the ink pen.

*Lobelia features on the corner of the small place cards, with polynathus and clematis leaves on the front left-hand card. All you need to do is follow the steps and you, too, can create these attractive gift cards.*

### Step Two
Trim any excess foliage from the pressed flowers you have chosen for this card.

### Step Three
Draw an outline of the flower design on the card, centering the design as in the photograph. Using tweezers, place each flower and its attached foliage in the center of the card and move each piece around until you are happy with its shape.

### Step Four
Carefully, take the pieces off the card and place them to one side in the same pattern.

Spray the card with adhesive and, using tweezers, replace the flowers onto the card. Press firmly into place, using a sheet of paper between your hand (or whatever you are using to press) and the arrangement. Leave to dry.

## Project Five
# A BEAUTIFUL BASKET

This project shows you how to create a basket full of pressed flowers. You can make the basket from moss and leaves as we have shown in the series of illustrations or from strong card, as in the photograph of the finished project.

The colors chosen for this arrangement are a combination of pink and purple, with a dash of cream and green foliage. Before you begin the creative process, look at the space where you are going to hang it and decide what proportion the finished item is to be. For example, a small and thin wall space requires a small arrangement in the same proportions (ie, small and thin) otherwise it will overpower the space and look out of place.

A large and wide space requires an arrangement that seems to take up all of the space, joyfully overflowing the basket almost onto the wall.

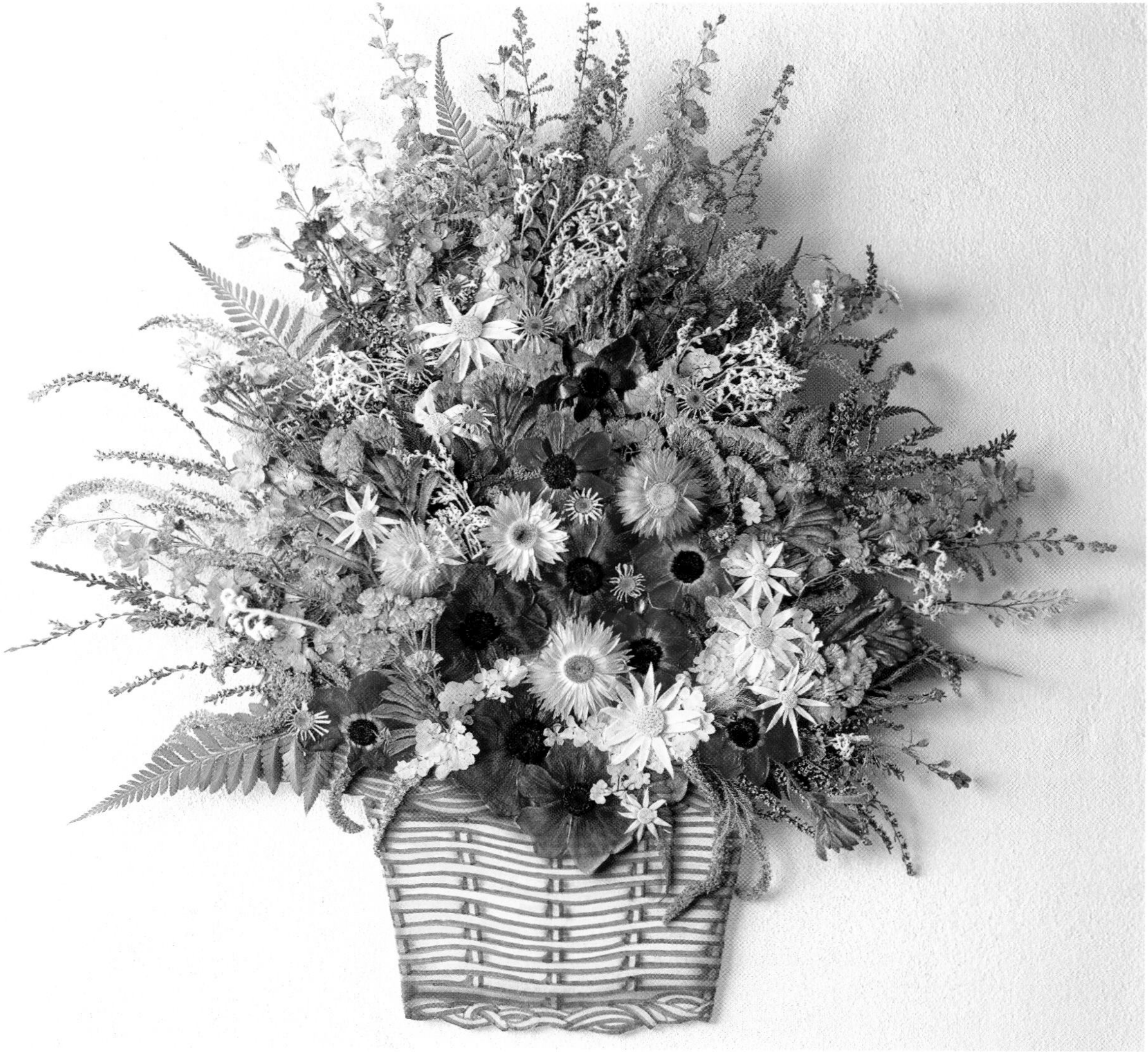

## MATERIALS

Adhesive

Collection of chosen pressed flowers

Fronds of fern (optional)

Moss (optional)

Card for a mount for the completed arrangement

Strong card

Scissors

Tweezers

## METHOD

### Step One

Cut out the shape of the basket from a piece of strong card. Ensure its size is in proportion to your final arrangement - about a quarter of the complete height. If you are leaving it as card, draw in the decorative wicker pattern.

If you like a moss effect, apply a thin layer of adhesive to the card and attach the pieces of moss, building up to a thick mass. Work from left to right, pushing the moss firmly onto the glue as you work and covering the card completely.

*Opposite:*
*The completed basket overflowing with pressed flowers. The base is made of strong card and the basketweave is painted on to the card.*

*You may prefer to use raffia to weave the basket shape for the base of the pressed arrangement. Make sure the basket shape lies flat on the card and is in proportion to the height of the pressed flowers to be used.*

### Step Two

To add the fern fronds, apply a thin layer of adhesive to the back of each fern frond and, using the tweezers, place onto the moss in an upright direction, working left to right. Press firmly into place. To cover the bottom ends, place one fern frond across the bottom. Trim all of the fern frond ends neatly.

### Step Three

Lay each of the pressed flowers species for the arrangement in separate groups on the workbench. Cut the mount to size and glue the basket shape to the mount, ready to begin the outline of the pressed arrangement. Place the green foliage fronds in position as seen in the photograph. Add the longer stems next, filling in around the edges. Once you are happy with the placement, glue into place. Make sure you place some of the flowers over the edge of the basket as in the photograph of the completed project. It softens the edges and makes it look natural.

Step Four
Begin to fill in with the medium-length stems, creating a more dense layer.
Finally, add the full-bloom flower heads *en masse*, making a focal point.
Once you are happy with the arrangement, glue into place. Leave to dry
and frame appropriately. Hang on the wall with a picture hook.

*The final arrangement is
a wonderful collection in
a country-style basket.*

# ACKNOWLEDGEMENTS

Editorial contributors: 'Fresh Flower Arranging' by Susan McAffer, with additional floral project bouquets by Sandy James Flowers; 'Dried Flower Arrangements' by Lynn Bryan, with additionl projects by Gillian Wimperis; and 'Pressed Flowers' by Christine Whiston, with additional project material by Nancy Henry. Additional text by Lynn Bryan. Thanks to James and Madeline for project, and Clive Nichols for garden and plant specimen photographs. Cover photograph by Di lewis.

# INDEX